Glowing Comments From
Aviation Experts About ...

AMELIA EARHART
-CASE CLOSED?

by
Walter Roessler & Leo Gomez

"A must read for anyone seeking a solution to one of the 20th century's most controversial mysteries — the disappearance of Amelia Earhart. Roessler and Gomez build their case, fact-by-fact, for a riveting account of exactly what happened."

> — **Doris Rich, Author**
> **Amelia Earhart - A Biography**

"I was impressed with Roessler and Gomez's book on Amelia Earhart. As a factual account of Amelia's journey, the attention to detail really pays off for the reader. As an aviator, it gave me a feel for what her adventure was like. The authors give us the facts and an account detailed and readable enough to take the trip along with AE; to be in the cockpit with her and actually hear the sound of the engines and propellers. For anyone interested in AE's incredible odyssey and disappearance, this book is the place to start. It is readable, it is interesting, and I couldn't put in down!"

> — **Patty Wagstaff**
> **National Aerobatic Champion**

"Brilliant...fascinating...excellent...superb. I would certainly recommend this book to anyone...I believe Roessler and Gomez are right on track."

> — **Gene Nora Jessen**
> **Former VP of the 99's**

"Fascinating, hard-to-put-down reading...Roessler and Gomez make a good case while refuting a number of the most intriguing speculative theories."

> — **Tom Beneson**
> **Sr. Editor, *Flying Magazine***

"...an impressive piece of research by, for the first time, qualified aviation professionals, and it makes perfect logic."
— **Luis Marden, Chief,**
Foreign Staff (Ret.), *Nat'l Geographic*

"I would say that the conclusions made by the writers are probably the most accurate philosophy of what happened to Amelia and Noonan while trying to locate Howland Island. The historian, both aviation and non-aviation oriented, will find this story on Amelia and her last flight to be educational and heartwarming. Long gone are the heroes and heroines who single-handedly stirred the hearts and imagination of all people."
— **Paul Poberezny, Chairman & Founder**
Experimental Aircraft Assn.

"I found the book to be very intriguing reading. The hypothesis presented is certainly believable and provides a new alternative solution to the mystery of Amelia's disappearance. The book is technical in nature, providing background knowledge for the aviation novice, as well as sufficient depth for the aviation historian or professional."
— **Dr. Peggy Baty**
President & Founder
Women In Aviation, International

"The Earhart story was factual and very good. It contained all qualitative data."
— **Brig. Gen. Chuck Yeager (Retired)**
First To Break The "Sound Barrier"

"If you have read other books and articles, or nothing at all, about Amelia Earhart, I strongly recommend this book be your choice. The authors have reached the most logical conclusion to the Earhart saga. This book will enhance your knowledge and fire your interest. It is totally factual and free of technical errors ... a monumental accomplishment."
— **LCDR William J. Hackett (Retired)**
Aviation Consultant

AMELIA EARHART
-CASE CLOSED?

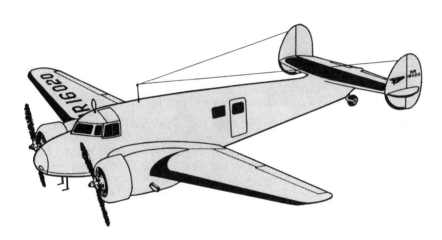

Walter Roessler & Leo Gomez
with Gail Lynne Green
Foreword by Patty Wagstaff, Nat'l Aerobatic Champion

An AViation Publishers Book
Published by Markowski International Publishers
Hummelstown, PA USA

AMELIA EARHART
-CASE CLOSED?

Walter Roessler & Leo Gomez
with
Gail Lynne Green

Published by

AVIATION PUBLISHERS
Markowski International Publishers
1 Oakglade Circle
Hummelstown, PA 17036 USA

Aviation Publishers is an imprint and trademark
of Markowski International Publishers

Manufactured in the United States of America

Publisher's Cataloging in Publication
(Prepared by Quality Books, Inc.)

Roessler, Walter
    Amelia Earhart - Case Closed?/Walter Roessler & Leo Gomez;
with Gail Lynne Green.

    p. cm. — (Historic aviation series)
    Preassigned LCCN: 95-79637.
    ISBN 0-938716-24-7 (pbk)
    ISBN 0-938716-25-5 (hc)

1. Earhart, Amelia, 1897-1937. 2. Aviation - History. 3. Women Air Pilots—United States—Biography. I. Gomez, Leo, II. Green, Gail Lynne. III. Title

TL540.3.R64 1996   629.13'092
                                    QBI95-20193

DEDICATION

To our wives, Vicky and Mary, for their
patience, understanding and moral
support, essential factors in the
achievement of this endeavor.

*"Please know I am
quite aware of the hazards.
I want to do it because
I want to do it. Women must
try to do things as
men have tried. When they fail,
their failure must be but a
challenge to others."*

AE

Fig. F-1. Amelia in her Canary with a gentle yet confident look of quiet determination. Part of a letter she wrote to her husband before leaving on a dangerous flight puts it all into words. See previous page. Photo courtesy Schlesinger Library, Radcliffe College.

High Flight

Oh, I have slipped the surly bonds of earth and danced the skies on laughter's silver wings. Sunward I have climbed and joined the tumbling mirth of sun-split clouds, and done a hundred things you have not dreamed of. Wheeled and soared and swung high in the sunlit silence. Hovering there, I have chased the shouting wind alone and flown my eagle craft through footless halls of air. Up, up the long, delirious burning blue, I have topped the wind-swept heights with easy grace where never lark or even eagle flew. And then, with silent lifting mind, I have trod the high, untrespassed sanctity of faith, put out my hand, and touched the face of God.

JOHN GILLESPIE MAGEE, JR.

A Personal Message From The Publisher

Over the years, a lot of "theories" concerning what happened to Amelia have been developed. With this book, the authors have done their "homework." Their objective was to find and tell the truth. They wanted to "set-the-record-straight," and we believe they have done so with "flying colors." You'll find no hearsay, inuendo, rumor or hype in this book — just the facts!

In working with the authors, we had a lot of "heart-to-heart" communications. Our common bond of a love of aviation and our admiration for Amelia made it easy. It's been an exciting experience and we hope you enjoy reading the book just as much as we did publishing it.

I've been "in love" with aviation all my life, perhaps as you have been. Even if you haven't however, you've probably heard about the "mysterious" disappearance of Amelia Earhart, the world's most famous woman pilot.

I have always been fascinated by "AE" and the great mystery that surrounded her and her attempt to fly around-the-world. I have always read magazine articles and books about her with great zeal. It has been exciting watching videos about her as well. I was continually inspired to learn more about her, while being awed by her courage.

Ever since I can remember, I have considered her in a league with Jackie Cochran, the Wright Brothers, Charles Lindbergh, and Chuck Yeager — trailblazers in aviation. She is definitely my aviation heroine of all time. I even memorized her poem "Courage," and have shared it often at motivational seminars. She was a "just-do-it" person. She knew what she wanted to do, and she did it!

Publishing this book has given us an even greater understanding of who she was and a true appreciation for what she did. We are more inspired than ever by her determination. Publishing this book has also given me the wonderful opportunity of communicating with the great aviation people who reviewed and commented on the original manuscript. It was special to be able to talk with them, and we feel honored by their participation. Their input certainly helped to make this book what it is.

We consider it an honor to be associated with Walter and Leo, and to publish this historically important work, which is a dream come true for me. May it help you better understand Amelia and what she accomplished for all of us. The next time you fly, especially over an ocean, maybe you'll think of this courageous woman named Amelia Earhart — "The First Lady of the Air."

Enjoy,
Mike Markowski

ACKNOWLEDGEMENTS

This work is a product of many fine people and organizations. We especially appreciate the contributions of photographs, materials, and historical and technical information, from the following:

To Gail Lynne Green, our "co-pilot," we give The Leather Helmet, Goggles and Fluttering White Scarf Award! She edited, wrote, rewrote, organized, re-organized, researched, word-processed, cajoled, supported, questioned, challenged, critiqued, encouraged, complimented and sent us "back-to-the-drawing-board" countless times. Her talent, craftsmanship and experience transformed our beginning draft into a book worthy of its subject.

To our publishers Mike and Marjie Markowski, whose devotion to producing the book was surpassed only by their love for aviation. Without their literary and publishing skills, and Mike's experience as an aeronautical engineer and pilot, the world would never have had this book. They are more than publishers, they are teammates and friends in our quest to tell the world the truth.

To Patty Wagstaff for her review and comments, and taking the time to write a sincere, heartwarming Foreword.

To Amelia Earhart Elementary School Faculty and especially Ms. Sylvia Holcomb, Hialeah Dade County, Florida

To Dumont Aircraft Engines, Avon Park, Florida

To Hamilton Standard Propellers, East Hartford, Connecticut

To Lockheed Corporation, Marietta, Georgia

To National Archives and Records Service, Wash., D.C.

To National Transportation Safety Board (NTSB), Washington, D.C.

To Sentry Books, Inc., Granada Hills, California

To Terry Story Aviation, Inc., Avon Park, Florida

To World Wide Photos, Inc., New York, N.Y.

To Smithsonian National Air & Space Museum, Wash., D.C.

To Sever Center for Western History Research Los Angeles, CA 90007

To Schlesinger Library at Radcliffe College, Cambridge, MA.

To Connie Johnston and Pat Fetzer at KeyComp Typographic Services for going above and beyond the call of duty in getting the book ready for press.

To Bob Griffiths who's artistic talent gave this book the fine three-view and perspective drawings.

To Dana Rine and Jeanne Shayter for their great cover design work.

To Amelia Earhart and Fred Noonan whose passion for aviation had them do whatever it took to fly and gave their lives doing it.

To Bill Hannan for his fine original three-view drawing of Amelia's Kinner "Canary."

To Loretta Gragg, Executive director of the "ninety-Nines" International Woman Pilot's Organization for supplying us with their July 1987 edition of "The 99 News," which commemorated the 50th Anniversary of Amelia's disappearance.

To General Chuck Yeager, Peggy Baty, Paul Poberezny, Doris Rich and LCDR William Hackett for reviewing and commenting on the original manuscript. We appreciate the time you spent on it. You all helped us "fine-tune" the text with your suggestions. You enabled us to produce as accurate a book as possible. It just wouldn't be what it is if you hadn't contributed.

And finally to all the aviation pioneers, we owe a debt of gratitude for your ingenuity and enthusiasm which continues to this day and into the future.

IN REMEMBRANCE...

Thank you, Amelia, for your pioneering spirit and determination to venture into the unknown, paving the way for all who have followed.

Your heroic feats paved the paths of modern aviation. If only you could have lived to see how far we have flown.

We shall remember you.

Fig. F-2. Publicity photo of Amelia Earhart atop her L-10 *Electra* upon delivery from Lockheed Corporation, Burbank, California. Courtesy Lockheed Corporation.

CONTENTS

FOREWORD

Amelia Earhart was as American as apple pie. She is one of our most beloved heroines. She has fascinated the world for years with her special charm and vision. Decades after her disappearance, we are still intrigued with her exploits, her accomplishments, and her life.

"AE," as she was known by many, was on a mission, as are all great adventurers and goal achievers. Her mission was our mission and indeed, is an integral part of our culture. That mission is to blend common sense with extraordinary achievement, to combine forward thinking with daring, and to strive for accomplishment with bravery. Amelia accomplished that mission and that is her legacy.

During the 1950's and '60's when I was growing-up, role models weren't so designated, however Amelia was a role model for me nonetheless. People loved to call her the "female Lindbergh," perhaps to explain or justify how a woman could be so capable, confident, and motivated. It was often said that she was "ahead-of-her-time," but I believe she was "in-tune" with her time. She sensed the opportunities before her and took full advantage of them.

The reason Amelia is still considered so great, is that she forged ahead with her goals. She went up-against the odds that were in her way as a woman, particularly as a woman in aviation. She was able to look an interviewer or camera in the eye and talk about her journey and her mission, without apologies or excuses. She never sacrificed her personality, or lost her identity. She always maintained her womanhood and a certain sweetness while participating in what was considered a man's field of endeavor. She and many others knew she was a pilot, not just a woman pilot. She was able to transcend preconceived ideas about women in aviation, and advocated women doing other things that only men had done before. This was her gift to me as a woman, particularly in aviation, and indeed to all of us.

There has never been a shortage of theories about what remains one of the greatest mysteries of the 20th century —AE's disappearance in the South Pacific during the Lae-to-

Howland Island-leg of her around-the-world flight. Some are mystical, some are far-fetched, and some take a seemingly plausible approach; all of them fuel the fires of intrigue.

With impeccable qualifications as airframe and powerplant mechanics, pilots, and aviation experts, Roessler and Gomez took on a real challenge when they authored this book. Their result is a "reader-friendly," provocative volume that I could not put down. I felt like I was in the cockpit with Amelia! They present the facts, sharing the results of their intensive and well-documented research. As Amelia's life continues to inspire us, we are fortunate to have this new book that reveals the truth about her and her journey.

—Patty Wagstaff

INTRODUCTION

Consider the many conveniences and luxuries we enjoy as modern air travelers. We take for granted such things as pressurized passenger cabins and carry-on luggage compartments. We love first-class seating sections with all types of hot and cold drinks, and tasty food served by capable flight attendants. We can span an ocean or continent in a matter of hours, while enjoying a good movie or our own selection of music.

Air travel has become the safest means of transportation. We owe that to dedicated flight personnel who have reliable, extremely accurate navigation equipment at their disposal. Computers make most of the calculations needed for safe flying. Navigation and weather information are available to pilots and flight crews via satellites and 24-hour-per-day weather briefers. Updated flight charts called "sectionals" provide pilots with accurate airport, radio and terrain information enroute. Modern jet aircraft can easily fly above inclement weather. Also, systems found on modern passenger aircraft are "redundant," meaning they are duplicated and can take over if a main system fails.

Flying was not always this way. If it were not for a handful of aviation pioneers who dared to fly greater distances, at higher altitudes and ever-increasing speeds, we could easily still be on the ground. We could be traveling cross-country in trains and automobiles, and traversing the oceans by ship.

Who were these early American aviation pioneers? We can begin with the Wright brothers who proved, in 1903, after many years of trial and error, that man could attain, control and sustain powered flight. From that moment on, the sky and universe waited to be conquered.

Early aviators flew "outside-the-envelope" of safety. They made it possible for us, a half-century later, to go to the edge of the envelope of flight in safety and comfort. In the early days, pilots flew with limited knowledge as to where the edge of the "danger zone" of their equipment began.

In the 1920's and 1930's, a dedicated group of daring aviators emerged to open the frontiers of flying. They challenged their airplanes, the elements, and their odds for success. They pushed themselves beyond their limits and the limits of their aircraft and in many cases, lost their lives.

Following is a summary of only a few notable achievements, and the men and women who reached them, in the early days of aviation:

1. The first powered aircraft was called the *Flyer*, which was built and flown by Wilbur and Orville Wright in 1903. It was equipped with one 12 hp water-cooled engine which drove two rear-mounted pusher propellers.

2. On July 25, 1909, French aviator Louis Bleriot became the first man to fly across the English Channel, in his 25 hp Bleriot XI monoplane with a nose-mounted engine. His flight originated in Calais, France and ended in Dover, England. His flight time across the channel was just over a half-hour.

3. The first passenger-carrying flying boat was a Benoist, powered by a 75 hp rear-mounted pusher engine. The aircraft carried one passenger and the pilot. Its inaugural flight occurred on January 1, 1914, between Tampa and St. Petersburg, Florida.

4. Between 1919 and 1920, many first international flights were made. An American Curtiss NC-4 flying boat equipped with four 400 hp engines was the first airplane to fly the Atlantic Ocean. It's route stretched from Long Island to Newfoundland, then to the Azores, a short hop to Portugal and finally to Plymouth, England. It took place between May 13, and 16, 1919.

5. In May, 1923, John A. Macready and Oakley G. Kelly flew a U.S. Army Air Service Fokker T-2 monoplane from New York to San Diego, California. This first ever, non-stop trans-continental flight covered 2,520 miles and took 26 hours and 50 minutes.

6. Charles Lindbergh soloed the Atlantic Ocean in a single-engine 220 hp Wright-powered Ryan monoplane called the *Spirit of St. Louis*. Lindbergh flew it non-stop on May 20 and 21, 1927 from New York to Paris, a distance of 3,610 miles, in 33 hours and 30 minutes.

7. Australia's Sir Charles Kingsford Smith, holder of 11 world aviation records, was the first aviator to encompass the world while flying cumulative flight legs at various times.

8. The U.S. National Air Races first began on Labor Day, 1929. During the early 1930's, many speed records of 200, 300 and over 350 mph were set. Most of the air racing designs were of the low-wing monoplane configuration, which quickly replaced the bi-plane. A few of the best known names in pioneer air racing were: Doug Davis, Roscoe Turner, Benny Howard, Howard Hughes, Steve Wittman and Jimmy Doolittle.

9. In July, 1933, Wiley Post flew around the world in his high-wing, all wood, Lockheed "Vega" monoplane named the *Winnie Mae*. He completed the flight in 7 days, 18 hours and 19 minutes.

10. Like Amelia Earhart, another pair of equally famous women aviators broke many flying records. Amy Johnson flew from England to Australia in a de Havilland "Moth" bi-plane. Not satisfied with that record, she then flew from Japan to Russia. Later, with her aviator husband, James Mollison, she flew their twin-engine de Havilland *Dragon* from East to West across the Atlantic Ocean in July, 1933.

Another famous woman aviation pioneer was British-born Jean Batten. In 1931, she flew solo between New Zealand and Japan in a seaplane. Her many records included a solo flight in 1934 between England and Australia and back to England, a double journey. She flew solo in 1936 from Australia to London by way of Peking, China.

Amelia Earhart's flying records join those of other courageous fliers to whom we owe our utmost respect and gratitude. They were the trailblazers.

About Amelia Earhart — The World's Most Famous Woman Pilot

Amelia Mary Earhart was born in Atchison, Kansas on July 24, 1897, to Edwin Stanton Earhart, a lawyer, and Amy Otis, daughter of a prominent Kansas judge. Her father's legal career was disappointing, and the family traveled from city to city while Edwin struggled to support his family, including a second daughter, Muriel Grace, born in 1900.

Amelia grew into an idealistic, independent and adventuresome young woman. She graduated from Hyde Park High School in Chicago in 1916. The following year, in Toronto, she nursed Canadian soldiers wounded in World War I. Motivated toward a medical career, in 1919 she began her pre-medical training at Columbia University in New York. Although she did well in school, she decided to take a break and join her family in California, where she attended her first air show.

With that first experience as a spectator, Amelia's fascination with flying became the focal point of her ambition. In 1921, after she found a female flying instructor named Neta Snook, her father arranged for flying lessons. Amelia soloed later that same year, at the age of 22. She loved the daredevil lifestyle of her fellow pilots. She delighted in donning the trappings which would become so identified with the era—a well-worn leather flight jacket, khaki pants, boots and neck scarf, topped by a leather helmet and goggles.

Amelia bought her first airplane in 1922, and doggedly practiced her flight maneuvers. Her mind was soon occupied with thoughts of new aviation feats. However, when her parents divorced in 1924, Amelia interrupted her flight training, returned to the East Coast with her mother and sister, and resumed her studies at Columbia. Finally realizing that a medical career was not for her, she began teaching English for the extension program at Massachusetts University. Her earnings were meager, and she began working as a social worker at Denison House in Boston, nearer her mother's home.

A career in flying was closest to her heart, and she was inspired and challenged by Lindbergh's magnificent solo

Fig. F-3. Amelia on right and Anita (Neta) Snook, her flying instructor. They are standing in front of Amelia's "Canary," 1921, in California. Courtesy of Purdue University.

crossing of the Atlantic in 1927. She was contacted by George Palmer Putnam, head of G.P. Putnam Sons Publishing Company, who was seeking a female pilot having fortitude and writing skills to fly the Atlantic as a passenger. Putnam's success with Lindbergh's book had been so rewarding that he coveted a similar best-seller. He decided a woman's story was what he needed.

Amelia eagerly accepted Putnam's offer. On June 17, 1928, Amelia landed at Burry Port, Wales with pilot Bill Stultz at the controls of the *Friendship,* a tri-motored Fokker seaplane owned by Mrs. Frederick Guest of London.

After that triumph, Putnam became Amelia's manager, mentor and promoter. Amelia's book, *20 Hrs., 40 Mins.,* her story about the Atlantic flight, catapulted her to worldwide fame. She launched into a lecture tour and became aviation editor of *Cosmopolitan* magazine. Commercial ventures followed, including designing clothes for plane travel and sponsoring the Amelia Earhart Lightweight Airplane Luggage line, still sold today.

George Putnam, fascinated by Amelia's charm and determination (not to mention her commercial potential), pursued

Fig. F-4. Amelia's first airplane, the Kinner Canary.

her business interests and her person. Persisting after Amelia declined his many proposals, he prevailed, and they were married in 1931. Though it did not appear to be a love match, their union meshed common interests. George provided money and publicity for Amelia's flying ventures and she attracted the attention he craved as he enjoyed her public's adulation. Putnam sold his interest in the family publishing company and became a Paramount Pictures executive while promoting Amelia's career.

Amelia planned to duplicate Lindbergh's 1927 Atlantic flight, and five years later she became the first woman to fly the Atlantic solo, landing in an Irish pasture. Thereafter, her accomplishments became legendary as she quickly continued to compile a breathtaking series of flying records.

Fig. F-5. Amelia shows her love for power, speed, and beauty as she stands in front of her shiny new *Electra* and classic 1936 Cord roadster. Courtesy Purdue University.

In 1935, Amelia was invited by Purdue University to join their faculty as a counselor to women students. She became a champion for women's rights, encouraging her students to be strong, resourceful and self-reliant. With Purdue's financial support, she purchased a twin-engine Lockheed *"Electra"* to replace the single-engine Lockheed *"Vega"* in which she had established so many records. The *"Electra"* would enable her to attempt her crowning achievement, a flight around-the-world.

Amelia hired Paul Mantz, noted pilot and aviation innovator, to be her technical advisor. She soon began training in her new aircraft which carried the latest in radio and navigation equipment, much of it experimental. When Amelia and Mantz were satisfied she was ready, she selected the crew for her first world flight attempt. Captain Harry Manning and Commander Fred J. Noonan were chosen, along with Mantz.

In March 1937, the crew of four left Oakland, California for Hawaii, on the first leg of their East-to-West world flight. Landing successfully at Wheeler Field, they planned to continue on to Howland Island the next day. The *"Electra"* was moved to Luke Field, judged to have a better surface, and on takeoff the next morning, the *"Electra"* groundlooped, sustaining sufficient damage to warrant overhaul at the Lockheed factory back in Oakland. The flight was canceled.

Undeterred by this setback, Amelia waited only for repairs on the *"Electra"* before her second attempt. Despite the defections of Manning and Mantz from her crew, she decided to make the flight accompanied only by navigator Fred Noonan. Two months later, on May 20, 1937, Amelia Earhart and Fred Noonan left Oakland, California, flying West-to-East in an attempt to circle the world at the Equator.

As we know, on the second-to-last-leg of their journey between Lae, New Guinea and Howland Island in the South Pacific, Earhart and Noonan disappeared on July 2, 1937, just 22 days before Amelia's 39th birthday. They and their Lockheed *Electra* were never found.

Instead of the tumultuous reception planned by George Putnam in Oakland, in anticipation of Amelia's arrival at the end of her record-setting flight, the world was stunned by her loss. The would-be celebrants joined millions of mourners.

Amelia's fate created speculation for decades and engendered a throng of publicity-seekers and theorists who, even today, attempt to exploit her story.

Amelia Earhart's accomplishments in aviation still inspire young fliers today, and remain glowingly recorded in the history of man's and woman's exploration of our skies.

Amelia Earhart's Awards and Decorations

1928   Medal of Valor, City of New York, presented by Mayor Jimmy Walker; Medal from City of Toledo; Medal from City of Philadelphia, presented by mayor; Medal from Commonwealth of Massachusetts; Medallion from Le Lyceum Societe des Femmes de France of New York.

1929   Medal from American Society of Mechanical Engineers.

1932   Distinguished Flying Cross, presented by the Congress of the United States; Medal from City of Chicago, presented by Mayor Cermak; Mayor's Committee Medal, City of New York, presented by Mayor Jimmy Walker; Medal from Commonwealth of Massachusetts; Medal from Aero Club Royal de Belgique; Medal from Aero Club de France; Medallion from Le Comite France Amerique; Medallion from Columbia Broadcasting System.

1933   Medallion from Women's Roosevelt Memorial Association.

1935   Medal from Mexico: Union de Mujeres-Americanas.

Key to Atlantic City.
Key to City of Pittsburgh.
Mexico: Order of the Aztec Eagle.
French Legion of Honor.
Belgium Order of Leopold.

In addition to these awards and decorations, Amelia was a founder and the first President of the now famous Ninety Nines, Inc., the international women pilots organization.

Historical Record Flights
Made By Amelia Earhart

1928   June 17: First woman to fly across the Atlantic Ocean as a passenger in a Fokker tri-motored seaplane.

1929   August 24: Third place winner in the Women's California to Cleveland, Ohio air race.

1930   July 6: Established a woman pilot's speed record for a three-kilometer course: 181.18 mph.

1931   April 8: Established a world auto-gyro record altitude flight of 18,451 feet.

1932   May 20-21: First woman to fly solo across the Atlantic Ocean. It took her 14 hours, 56 minutes.

1933   July 7-8: Established a new trans-continental air speed record flying from California to New Jersey: 2,447.8 miles in 19 hours, 5 minutes.

1935   January 11-12: First woman to fly solo from Hawaii to California: 2,408 miles in 18 hours, 16 minutes.

1935   April 19-20: First woman to fly solo from California to Mexico City in 13 hours, 23 minutes.

About Fred Noonan — Amelia's Navigator

Fred Noonan was not Amelia Earhart's first choice for navigator for her world flight. Harry Manning was to have been first navigator, with Noonan assisting, but after Manning declined to continue with Amelia's second world flight attempt, Noonan became her logical second choice. The search for another qualified navigator, willing to assume the risks involved in the flight, might have taken costly weeks or months.

Newly-married, Noonan hesitated to take full responsibility for navigation. Even so, he hoped to share in the credit and publicity surrounding the flight to provide a boost to a future business venture. His decision was fatal.

Fred Noonan began his navigation career on the seas at a young age. He served on various commercial ships before joining the British Royal Navy during World War I. There, he distinguished himself by saving the lives of several Allied compatriots.

After the war, Noonan developed an interest in flying, and took flying lessons. Transferring his knowledge of sea navigation to the air, he became a commercial airlines navigation instructor. Pan American Airways hired him as a navigator. Later he became an instructor, as well as representing the airline at several locations around the world. He was navigator for the famous Pan American *China Clipper* when commercial trans-Pacific service began in 1935.

Amelia felt that Noonan, with his easy-going sense of humor and diverse experience, would be a compatible and competent companion on her world flight. He was in his early forties when their adventure began, and they shared a common love of flying. We will never know Noonan's thoughts and feelings during his last hours, but we do know of his courage. He was with Amelia until the end.

About Paul Mantz —
Amelia's Technical Advisor

Albert Paul Mantz was born in California in 1903. At the age of 16, he took his first flying lesson. Paul joined the Army Air Corps in 1927 and became an aviation cadet. With a military flight record of 126 hours and an evaluation rating of outstanding, he was washed out of the cadet program for "buzzing" (a low altitude zoom) a train carrying high ranking officers.

After he left the army, Mantz became one of the best known precision flyers of his day. He never considered himself a stunt pilot; every sequence he flew was carefully planned.

In the 1930's, he became a west coast distributor for Fleet aircraft and continued trying to break into the "closed circle" of Hollywood movie pilots. This was impossible, until Florence Lowe "Pancho" Barnes recognized his outstanding flying ability and drive. He eventually became Hollywood's top movie pilot and his leadership resulted in the formation of the Motion Picture Pilots Association.

Mantz ingratiated himself to become a confidant of major movie stars such as Clark Gable, Jimmy Stewart, John Wayne, Bob Hope and Tom Mix. He also owned and operated The Charter Service of the Stars and he called it the "Honeymoon Express." Other important people using this service were: first lady Eleanor Roosevelt, Presidential candidate Wendell Willkie, and movie director Alfred Hitchcock.

He became even more established after starting "United Air Services," which provided airplanes and pilots for motion picture studios. He was sought-after by many Hollywood studios looking for a pilot who was able to perform flying maneuvers no other pilot would attempt.

Mantz used many of his aircraft as "Flying Ambulances" helping those in need, sometimes at night and under the most severe conditions. He also dropped supplies to forest fire fighters and using chemicals and dry ice, "seeded" cumulonimbus clouds to produce rain in dry locations when nature failed.

Amelia Earhart Putnam was a contemporary and close friend of Paul Mantz and she looked to him for technical advice to prepare her for the "World Flight" in her **new twin-engine** Lockheed *Electra*. At his United Air Services hanger, Mantz trained Amelia in long-range navigation, multi-engine procedures and instrument flying. Paul also hired experts to design and install some special equipment in Amelia's *Electra* such as the crossfeed fuel system and he then worked with her on becoming completely familiar with modifications to it.

Mantz also planned and supervised every phase of Amelia's world flight. He even accompanied her, along with navigators Harry Manning and Fred Noonan, on the first leg of the flight from California to Hawaii on March 17, 1937.

In 1935, Paul and Amelia agreed to start the Earhart-Mantz flying school, but their plans were not to be finalized.

In September 1942, Paul Mantz left a $66,000 a year profession to accept a commission of Major in the U.S. Army Air Corps and take command of the first motion picture unit (FMPU) during the second World War. Some Hollywood movie actors serving under Mantz were Clark Gable, Alan Ladd, Ronald Reagan, George Montgomery, Van Helflin and Arthur Kennedy, in addition to many motion picture and combat photographers. His unit turned out some 300 training films and shot some 300,000 feet of aerial combat sequences. In 1943, Mantz was promoted to Lt. Colonel and flew with noted military flyers such as General Jimmy Doolittle, General Hap Arnold, General Chuck Yeager, and noted aviators Jackie Cochran and Roscoe Turner.

After the war, Mantz resumed his charter service. Lowell Thomas, world traveler and explorer, hired him to film his famous "Cinerama" film series in the United States and around the world. Mantz developed the multi-camera techniques for these films and personally directed filming from a chair in the nose of a converted B-25 World War II bomber. The plane was fitted with optically clear glass. The 360 degree movie screen now shown at Disney World theme parks is the product of Paul Mantz aerial photography and camera skills.

Some of the more famous flying movies Mantz directed were, "12 O'Clock High," "West Point Of The Air," "Test Pilot," "Flying Tigers," "The Spirit of St. Louis" and the "Flight Of The Phoenix." There were many more, too numerous to mention.

Paul Mantz's Flying Awards and Record Flights

1. On July 6, 1930 in San Mateo, California, he flew 46 consecutive outside loops.

2. He personally won three air races in Chicago on Labor Day in 1933.

3. He placed third in aerobatic competition in St. Louis, Missouri in May of 1937 after receiving only thirty minutes of verbal instruction on the ground by fellow aviator Tex Rankin.

4. He placed third in the 1938 Bendix Air Race flying an Oran Shell Lightning.

5. He placed third again in the 1939 Bendix Air Race, once again flying the Oran Shell Lightning.

6. He won the Bendix Trophy for the years 1946, 1947 and 1948 using a modified P-51 Mustang with an Allison engine.

7. He flew from Los Angeles, California to Houston, Texas in 3 hours, 6 minutes and 36 seconds.

8. He flew from Houston, Texas to Mexico City in 2 hours, 10 minutes and 5 seconds.

9. He flew from Mexico City to Burbank, California in 4 hours, 15 minutes and 45 seconds.

10. He flew from Burbank, California to New York City in 4 hours, 52 minutes and 58 seconds.

Paul Mantz was also the recipient of the Air Force Association award for excellence for his work in Cinerama aerial movies. After Amelia Earhart's disappearance, Mantz continued his impressive career, fulfilling a 20 year dream of founding a museum of aviation memorabilia.

Paul Mantz was killed while flying the dummy plane he had built for the movie titled "The Flight Of The Phoenix," staring Jimmy Stewart. This picture was shot in 1966 and he had said it would be his "last stunt;" unfortunately it was.

PRELUDE

Probably few people are aware that in Hialeah, Florida, across the street from the old, de-activated Amelia Earhart Flying Field, where the Hialeah Police Department and Hialeah Public Works are now located, there stands a modern elementary school and a 515-acre park and recreational facility, both named in memory of Amelia Earhart.

While doing research for this book, I began to reminisce about my daily encounters with the busts of Amelia Earhart and Charles Lindbergh located in the lobby of Silver Bluff Elementary School in Miami. During a trip to Miami, I decided to make a sentimental digression to my old elementary school to see if the busts of Amelia and Charles were still in the lobby.

Fig. F-6. Amelia Earhart Elementary School, Hialeah, Florida. Gomez photo.

Fig. F-7. Amelia Earhart Recreational Park, Hialeah, Florida. Gomez photo.

In June of 1988, 57 years after my elementary school days, I entered the Silver Bluffs Elementary School with a natural feeling of nostalgia. The Earhart and Lindbergh busts were gone, and no-one I spoke to could recall their existence. However, one of the teachers suggested they might possibly be found at the Amelia Earhart Elementary School in Hialeah.

At Amelia Earhart Elementary School, I hoped not only to locate the sculptures, but also to gather material for our book. I photographed the commemorative plaques, pictures and signs dedicated to Amelia Earhart's memory.

No one at the school could help in locating the missing busts, but I did meet some interesting people. I explained to the Librarian, Mrs. Elizabeth Gould, that I would appreciate any information that would help us research our book. In turn, Mrs. Gould introduced me to the school principal, Mrs. Patsy M. Mason.

Mrs. Mason was delighted to cooperate, and she directed me to Mrs. Sylvia Holcomb, who was, coincidentally, about to retire from teaching that very day. At her invitation, I spent some time in her classroom, and when Mrs. Holcomb told the children I was visiting to talk about Amelia Earhart, quiet presided in the room. Just the mention of Amelia's name held the children spellbound.

Later, Mrs. Holcomb told me her mother was Sara Andrews, who once worked at Hatcher's Restaurant, across the street from the old flying field. It was then called Miami Municipal Airport and later changed to Amelia Earhart Field in her memory. At Hatcher's Restaurant, Sara Andrews served Amelia's meals whenever she stopped there. Amelia always had one of her favorites, a large glass of buttermilk with bits of butter floating in it. Amelia was fond of the restaurant and often dined there during her eight-day stay in Miami. This was prior to her departing for Puerto Rico on the first over-water leg of her second world flight attempt. Mrs. Holcomb shared that her mother had prepared the lunch for Amelia's San Juan flight.

Fig. F-8. A plaque found at Amelia Earhart Elementary School. Gomez photo.

Fig. F-9. Another plaque found at Amelia Earhart Elementary School. Gomez photo.

Mrs. Holcomb said, "I always had a soft spot in my heart for Amelia Earhart," whom she called a "great lady." She spoke about a P.T.A. meeting at the school in 1984 when one of the honored guests was Cynthia Putnam Trefelner, daughter of Amelia's stepson and friend of school librarian Elizabeth Gould. Mrs. Trefelner commented during the meeting that "there was no stopping this woman," referring, of course, to her late step-grandmother, Amelia Earhart Putnam.

I had spent a very pleasant day at the school, but the whereabouts of the busts were still unknown. The trail was cold.

Later, though, the trail began to heat up. My brother, John Gomez, remembered during one of our conversations that the busts were sculpted by the brother of one of the elementary school teachers, a Ms. Skinner. I found Ms. Skinner's home in Coconut Grove, Florida, and its current owner, Mrs. Post, solved my mystery — or at least part of it. In Mrs. Post's garden, I found the "lost" bust of Amelia Earhart prominently displayed. Unfortunately, the bust of Lindbergh was stolen.

— Leo F. Gomez

Fig. F-10. Painting of Amelia Earhart displayed in the school office at Amelia Earhart Elementary School. Gomez photo.

Fig. F-11. "Misplaced" bust of Amelia Earhart was located, then photographed, in Mrs. Post's yard. Gomez photo.

"What kind of man would live where there is no daring? I don't believe in taking foolish chances, but nothing can be accomplished without taking any chance at all."

CHARLES LINDBERGH

"He who tries and fails may, in himself, be a greater hero than is the one for whom the band played."

AMELIA EARHART

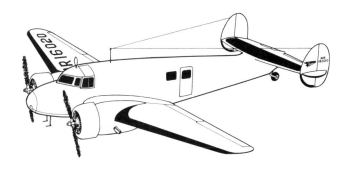

Chapter One

AMELIA FLIES THE OCEANS

Her "Little Red Bus" Served Her Well

Prior to the first attempt by Amelia Earhart and navigator Fred Noonan to fly around the world in their Lockheed *Electra* in 1937, Amelia had successfully flown across the Atlantic Ocean, the Pacific Ocean from Hawaii-to-Oakland, and then across the Gulf of Mexico. These three ocean crossings bolstered her courage and prepared her for the greatest flight of her career—circumnavigation of the earth at its greatest distance. We will briefly cover these three flights mainly to illustrate that the propellers used on Earhart's *Wasp* engine were either the fixed-pitch type or the two-position controllable type. These propellers, previously described, required little or no attention on the part of the pilot.

1932 Solo Atlantic Crossing

In 1929, Amelia Earhart became the first woman pilot to fly across the Atlantic Ocean. However, she was only a passenger on that flight aboard the tri-motored seaplane called the *Friendship*. She was determined that one day she would attempt the same crossing solo.

That day finally came during the third week of May, 1932. Amelia took off in a Lockheed *Vega* from Teterboro Airport in New Jersey. The *Wasp* powered single-engine *Vega* was flown with a ground adjustable, fixed-pitch propeller. She had no autopilot or DF navigational equipment on board.

The pitch was fixed at a pre-determined angle. It would take the best of the engine's power, depending on the required performance; high rpm (low pitch) was used for maximum power during takeoff and climb, while low rpm (high pitch) was used for cruising. Since no pitch changes were possible from the cockpit, all Amelia had to concern herself with was her engine rpm settings. She could therefore spend more time concentrating on navigation and weather problems.

Amelia soloed across the Atlantic Ocean. However, instead of landing at her intended destination airport, she set down in an Irish cow pasture! Nevertheless, she had once again defied the odds. She became the first woman pilot to cross the Atlantic Ocean solo, after Charles Lindbergh's flight in May of 1927.

Fig. 1-1. Amelia was mobbed after completing the first solo flight from Hawaii to the United States, 1935. Everybody loved her! Courtesy Purdue University.

1935 Solo Pacific Crossing, Hawaii to California

On January 11, 1935, Amelia Earhart, once again flying her Lockheed *Vega* equipped with a dependable Pratt and Whitney *Wasp* engine and new controllable two-position propeller, took off from Wheeler Field in Hawaii bound for Oakland, California, 2400 miles away. Neither an autopilot or DF navigational equipment were aboard.

The new propeller used on this flight gave Amelia the ability to adjust the pitch from within the cockpit to low-pitch (high rpm) for takeoff or high-pitch (low rpm) for cruising. The advantage over the fixed-pitch propeller was obvious. Maximum takeoff power was transmitted directly to the propeller via its most efficient blade setting, lifting a heavily loaded aircraft as quickly as possible off the ground. Amelia carried a lot of extra fuel for this long flight and the advantage of changing to high-pitch while cruising provided the best fuel economy.

Fig. 1-2. Artist's sketch of Amelia's "Little Red Bus."

Gulf of Mexico Flight

On April 19, 1935, Amelia Earhart flew solo from Burbank, California-to-Mexico City, 1700 miles away. She then flew 2,185 miles to Newark, New Jersey, 700 of those miles over the Gulf-of-Mexico. Because she had access to numerous known locations of commercial radio stations, navigation on this flight was relatively easy.

She again used her Lockheed *Vega* and two-position controllable pitch propeller for these long distance flights. Amelia's three solo over-water flights strengthened her resolve for a world flight.

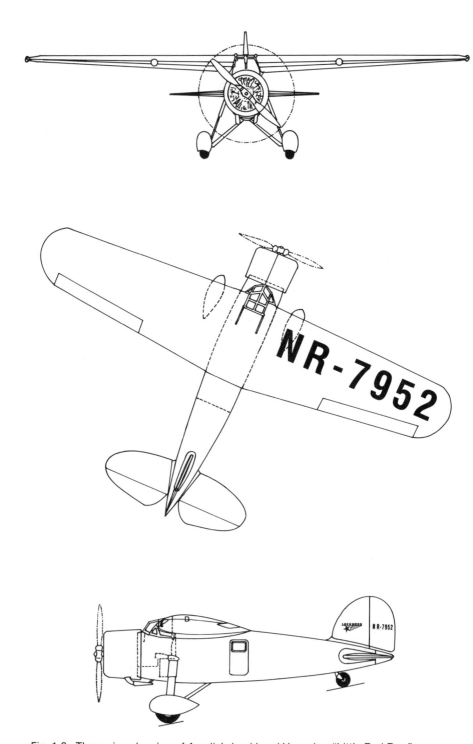

Fig. 1-3. Three-view drawing of Amelia's Lockheed Vega; her "Little Red Bus."

First Woman to Cross North Atlantic (Passenger)

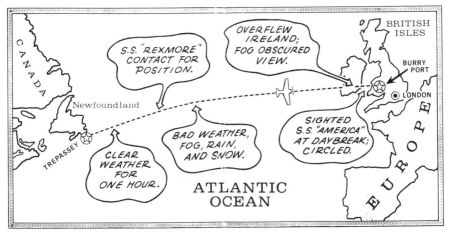

AMELIA EARHART - ROUTE AS PASSENGER - 1928

Fig. 1-4. Amelia first flew the Atlantic as a passenger. NASM map.

First Woman to Fly the Atlantic (Solo)

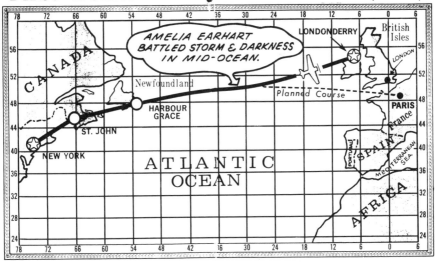

AMELIA EARHART ROUTE ACROSS ATLANTIC - 1932

Fig. 1-5. Amelia flew the Atlantic solo to duplicate Lindbergh's historic flight. NASM map.

First Woman to Fly From Hawaii to Mainland USA

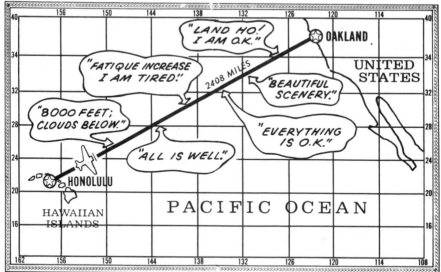

AMELIA EARHART ROUTE ★ HONOLULU to OAKLAND - 1935

Fig. 1-6. Amelia was the first woman to fly from Hawaii to mainland United States. NASM map.

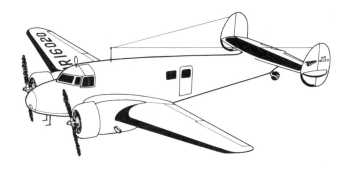

Chapter Two

AMELIA'S FLYING LABORATORY
The Latest Technology
To Make Her Flight Easier

Dispelling the Myth—No More Rumors, Lies, or Hype

This book is not based on speculation. Everything you are about to read is derived from factual information. It was obtained after several years of detailed research and over 80 years of combined aviation experience, including 30 years of U.S. Navy flying by Lieutenant Commander William J. (Bill) Hackett.

We believe these facts will "once-and-for-all" solve one of the 20th Century's greatest mysteries. How and why did Amelia Earhart, navigator Fred Noonan and their Lockheed *Electra* NR-16020 disappear on July 2, 1937? How come they didn't reach Howland Island, midway between Lae, New Guinea and Hawaii during their around-the-world flight?

We have personally flown, maintained and operated aircraft, autopilots, instruments, propellers and engines identical or similar to those used by Amelia Earhart in 1937. In order to understand the monumental odds faced by Amelia on her around-the-world flight attempts, it is important to comprehend the operation of a few pieces of essential aircraft equipment. Much of this equipment was quite new in the 1930's, and it was mandatory that it function perfectly if Earhart's objective was to be accomplished. A world flight of 28,000 miles would severely test Amelia and her airplane. If they failed, the flight would fail.

Equipment operation is discussed in this chapter. We have described, as clearly and simply as possible, how equipment played a critical role in the mystery of Amelia Earhart's disappearance. As a matter of interest, we have included a history of similar updated equipment used in aircraft after those flown by Earhart, up to the last successful internal combustion aircraft engine.

Amelia's choice for her dangerous, long-range flight was the Lockheed *Electra*, a very capable 10-passenger, twin-engine, dual-control transport. It was "big brother" to the Lockheed *Ventura* PV-1 and other Lockheed aircraft which we later piloted or in which we crewed. The *Electra* would be Amelia's "safety bridge." It was powered by two 550 hp Pratt and Whitney S3H1-1340 *Wasp* engines and boasted newly-developed Hamilton Standard constant speed propellers. It also featured a recently developed radio directional finder reported as non-rotatable (commonly known as a "DF") and a newly developed Sperry automatic pilot. The aircraft had a wingspan of 55 feet and a fuselage length of 41 feet.

To provide Amelia with the longest possible flying range, custom-made gasoline tanks were installed. There were six in the main cabin and three in each wing, for a total capacity of 1,202 gallons of gasoline weighing 7,813 pounds. Fuel carried in the cabin alone weighed 5,226 pounds. At a burn rate of 50 gallons per hour, this amount of fuel would have given Earhart and Noonan 24 hours of flying time between stops.

Paul Mantz, Amelia's technical advisor, personally consulted with all manufacturers involved in modifications to her *Electra* for her long-range flights. Every effort was made to equip the aircraft with state-of-the-art (at that time) instruments for the arduous flights she had planned.

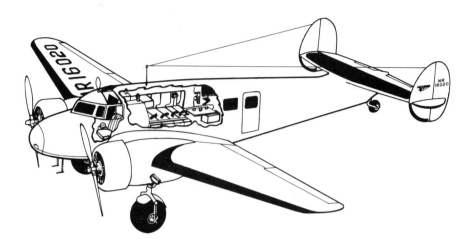

Fig. 2-1. Cutaway drawing of Amelia's *Electra* showing cockpit, fuselage fuel tanks, and navigator's station. Bob Griffiths drawing.

To assure success, Amelia needed dependable, along-the-route backup support and proper operation of all the newly-developed equipment on board the *Electra*. No redundancy (backup equipment which is now used on modern aircraft) was installed on Amelia Earhart's airplane. In light of current aviation technology, it is no wonder Amelia's feats have become part of the legends and lore of aviation history.

Early Propellers

In the early days of aviation, airplane propellers were made of wood, and the pitch or blade angle was fixed; it could not be changed. The propeller converted the engine's power to thrust, which in turn moved the airplane on the ground and through the air. Fixed blade angles were most efficient at only one airspeed, which compromised an airplane's performance at other airspeeds. This would be like a car with only one gear!

Blades were designed and fixed in the low pitch position for lifting heavy loads off the ground in as short a distance as possible. They were fixed in the high pitch position where short distance takeoff was not as critical as fuel economy. The drawback of the high-pitch position was reduced performance at lower aircraft speeds, particularly rate of climb.

Ground Adjustable Pitch Propellers

The blades of adjustable pitch propellers could be changed on the ground prior to engine start. The angles could be adjusted to either the low or high pitch position by rotating them at the hub and then locking them in place. Their angle was set depending on the performance sought.

Controllable Pitch Propellers

This type of propeller was first used commercially in the mid-1930's. Designed to allow the pilot to control the blade angle settings from the cockpit, a two-position propeller control could move the blades, while running, to either the low or high-pitch positions. For example, you could set the blade angle of the propeller to the low-pitch position for takeoff. Upon reaching the desired cruising altitude, you could then move the blades to high-pitch for most economical fuel consumption. This was like shifting a car into high gear or overdrive!

In the photo on the next page, note that the two-position, controllable pitch propeller on Amelia's Lockheed *Vega* Wasp engine was left in the low-pitch position. This exposed the pitch changing pistons to the elements, which could cause corrosion and lead to a malfunction and incipient failure during a later-required propeller pitch change. Amelia's failure to change to the high pitch setting after a flight and prior to engine shutdown (standard operating procedure), may have indicated she had established a habit that would later cause equipment problems. Prior to this flight, she had used either a fixed-pitch or a ground-adjustable-pitch propeller, neither of which required attention by the pilot prior to engine shutdown!

The following information on constant speed propellers is extremely important. It played a major part in the Luke

Fig. 2-2. Amelia being welcomed by an enthusiastic public in Oakland, California, after her solo non-stop flight from Hawaii in 1935. Her Lockheed *Vega* has a two-position controllable pitch propeller. National Archives photo.

Field, Hawaii groundloop accident of Amelia's Electra during her takeoff from that field (authors' italics).

Constant Speed Propeller

After the controllable-pitch propeller was placed into operation, the propeller governor appeared. It was known as a *constant speed* control mechanism that allowed infinite adjustments of pitch, while in operation! It was invented by Hamilton Standard in collaboration with the experienced Woodward Governor Company. The year was 1935 and these were the same propellers Amelia used on her *Electra*.

The governor controlled the flow of engine oil toward and away from the propeller by counterweights spinning in the governor, and by an adjustable engine driven valve. Low-pitch was used for takeoff. When cruising altitude was reached, the pitch could be adjusted to obtain any desired RPM and thereby increase efficiency and performance.

For example, let's say you wanted to hold 1,950 RPM and 33 inches of manifold pressure (power). You'd simply adjust the propeller until you read 1,950 RPM; then adjust the throttle to the desired manifold pressure. The engine would deliver the best fuel efficiency while still running at the same RPM; from then on! Regardless of the altitude of the airplane, whether climbing, diving, turning or flying into denser or thinner air — no matter what conditions were encountered, the engine would still turn at 1,950 RPM. Constant power would be delivered to the propeller at all times, unless the manifold pressure was changed by selecting a different throttle setting.

The early Hamilton Standard constant speed propeller proved to be a critical innovation in the evolution of powered flight. This breakthrough gave us the equivalent of a gear box, functioning similarly to the transmission of your car. For example, if you were to start a stick shift car in high gear, the vehicle would hardly get moving. In fact, you could easily stall the engine. However, when you shift the transmission into low-gear for starting out, and then to each succeeding gear as you accelerate, the car's speed increases smoothly as you go. The constant speed propeller gave us the capability to, in effect, change "gears" (blade angles) for takeoff, climb, cruise and landing.

Navy regulations covering the maintenance of these propellers were strictly enforced. Prior to shutting-down the engine, the propeller was always to be placed in the high-pitch, lower rpm position. This was required to prevent the steel pitch change pistons from rusting when left uncovered in the low-pitch position. It would increase oil seal wear and also cause the propeller to fling oil all over the engine, cowling and windshield. The aluminum cylinder protected the piston only when the propeller was shut down in the high-pitch position. The piston was exposed when the prop was in low-pitch, which would normally be a very short period of time during a climb or descent.

In Fig. 2-3, again, the counterweights are fully retracted, indicating the propeller is in the low-pitch, high rpm position. Apparently, Amelia did not place too much importance on

Fig. 2-3. Amelia Earhart standing on the wing of her Lockheed *Electra* in Miami, Florida, early in her second world flight attempt, May, 1937. Note constant speed propeller in low-pitch! National Archives photo.

this critical shutdown position. It is also possible that, because constant speed propellers were relatively new in 1937, many pilots may not have been totally aware that the exposed steel piston would rust, causing oil leaks and pitch control problems.

The early model constant speed propeller was not perfect by any means. When Amelia used the relatively new prop on her *Electra* in 1937, it was one of the few aircraft of that period actually using the governor-controlled device. She had never used it before and was also new at flying twin-engine aircraft.

Prior to the constant speed propeller, most aircraft were using either fixed-pitch or two-position props. The difference in the new design was that the entire pitch range could be controlled, not just the high and low-pitch settings, as with the controllable pitch prop.

During the 1940's, co-author Leo F. Gomez was a Navy airplane captain. He maintained and flew the OS2U-3 *Kingfisher*, a single-engine seaplane observation scout used primarily to escort military convoys out to sea from New York Harbor. His squadron was stationed at Floyd Bennett Field on the shores of Jamaica Bay in Brooklyn, New York.

The OS2U-3 was equipped with a Pratt and Whitney *Wasp* R-985 engine and a Hamilton Standard constant speed propeller. Probably the most severe result of lack of proper maintenance and operation on the pitch piston was that it would tend to stick. If your propeller was stuck in an inefficient pitch, especially out over the open sea, your engine would consume more fuel than planned. You could run out before reaching your destination and, of course, have to ditch the airplane in the water!

During his tour of duty, Gomez personally responded to downed *Kingfisher* Naval aircraft frozen in pitch. This occured twice within sight of the Ambrose Lighthouse ship. He had to transfer fuel from his aircraft over to the disabled aircraft by using a hand-operated wobble pump. Accomplishing this in three-foot swells between two bobbing and weaving seaplanes was certainly no fun. If the downed aircraft had been a land plane instead of a seaplane, it would undoubtedly have sunk!

Surprisingly, there are still some Hamilton Standard constant speed propellers in service to this day. A typical example would be the Grumman *AG-CAT* crop duster, powered with a Pratt and Whitney *Wasp* R-1340 engine. These specially built aircraft use the same engine and propeller combination as did Amelia Earhart's 1937 Lockheed *Electra*, except for a few important differences. The newer engines have greatly improved metals, and are more reliable. Furthermore, the pitch change pistons are now <u>chromeplated</u>, reducing the possibility of rust and a stuck blade angle.

Hydromatic Constant Speed Propeller

A great improvement over the constant speed propeller was the Hydromatic constant speed propeller. It accomplished the same things, but with one major difference. A dome over the hub, completely covered the pistons, cylinders and oil seals. This eliminated the rust and oil leak problems so frequently encountered before. Propeller maintenance time was greatly reduced, and the Hydromatic rarely stuck in pitch.

Turbo Engine Driven Propeller

Many of today's propellers have a self-contained filtered oil system and are driven by turbine engines. They no longer depend on engine oil for pitch changes. Through years of constant improvement, the modern propeller has become an efficient, reliable part of the aircraft. When properly maintained, the failure rate is greatly reduced, if not eliminated.

Propeller Progress

Propellers continually advanced from fixed-pitch all the way through to Hydromatic constant speed. A typical example of this progression can be found on Douglas DC-1, DC-2 and DC-3 twin-engine aircraft.

The DC-1 had ground-adjustable, fixed-pitch, three-bladed Hamilton Standard propellers. The first flight of the DC-1 with this type occurred on July 1, 1933.

The DC-1 was given the nickname *Gooney Bird* because, like its namesake, it required a long takeoff run. The propellers were fixed in the cruise pitch position for efficient cross-country flying, at the sacrifice of short takeoff runs and higher climb rates.

The DC-2 was introduced in 1934 and had controllable pitch props. The pilot could manually select either low or high-pitch making it possible to use the best blade angle for either takeoff or cruise.

In 1935, the Douglas DC-3 was introduced with Hamilton Standard constant speed propellers and governors. The DC-3 and its military versions, the C-47 and R4D, were used extensively for passenger, troop carrier and cargo missions. This helped considerably in winning World War II. By the

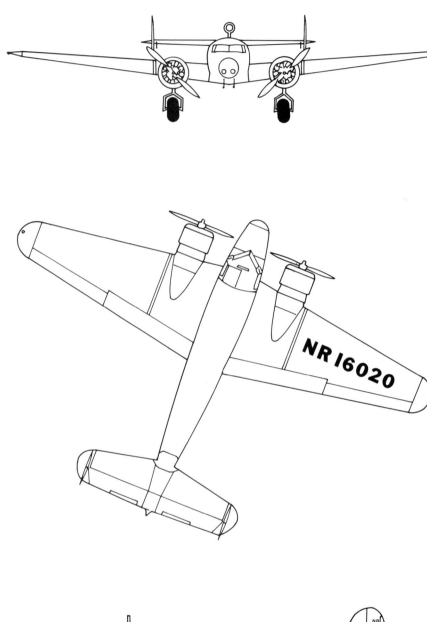

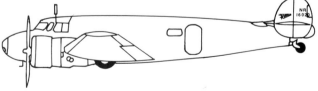

Fig. 2-4. Three-view drawing of Amelia's Lockheed *Electra*.

Fig. 2-5. The pitch change pistons and cylinders are protected by a hub dome on this DC-3's Hydromatic constant speed prop. Courtesy Sentry Books, Inc.

early 1940's both the Douglas DC-3 and its military counterparts were equipped with the new Hamilton Standard Hydromatic constant speed propeller. In addition to improving efficiency they could also be "feathered." This meant the pilot could set the blade angle for minimum air resistance in the event of an engine failure. Truly an advantage for multi-engined aircraft. Furthermore, if they were shut down in low (wrong)-pitch, they couldn't rust!

Although the Hamilton Standard propellers continued to improve the performance of the DC-1's, DC-2's, and DC-3's, the nickname *Gooney Bird* sticks with the airplane, even to this day!

The Automatic Pilot

The Sperry Autopilot used by Amelia Earhart in 1937 was one of the earliest developments of the automatic pilot. At that time, it was one of the most reliable pieces of equipment that could take over the controls of an aircraft in flight. It was designed to keep the aircraft reasonably "straight-and-level" while also maintaining the desired heading. Early autopilots, however, had a number of limitations. They required continuous monitoring while engaged and in control of the aircraft.

Gyros were the heart of the autopilot. Unfortunately, they had two troublesome characteristics: (1) **rigidity,** which maintained the instrument as a stable device, and (2) **precession,** which caused the instrument to "drift" because of friction within the bearings and suspending devices.

The autopilot used by Amelia Earhart aboard her *Electra* had the tolerances actually allowed on the workbench of the instrument overhaul shop, and in the manufacture of the instrument itself. The "artificial horizon" part of the autopilot instrument was more tolerant of internal friction. It contained a pendulous vane assembly that hung down off the bottom of

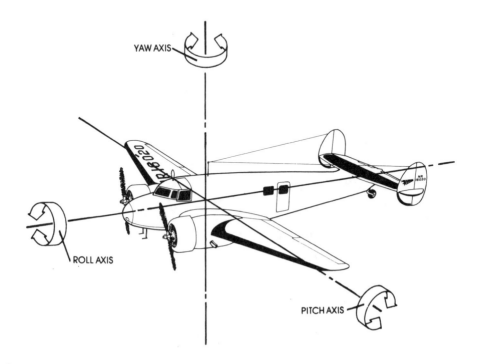

Fig. 2-6. An airplane has three axes of rotation.

Fig. 2-7. Amelia Earhart at the controls of her Lockheed *Electra*. National Archives photo.

the gyro housing. It kept the gyro straight and erect with the horizon. The directional gyro of the autopilot did not have this feature because it was free-suspended. You had to reset or "cage" it every 15 minutes to stay on course; otherwise you would eventually fly in a continuous circle. Obviously, a pilot flying with this directional gyro could not afford to become lax in its observation, especially on a long flight.

Autopilot instruments on modern airliners have a tolerance of only .007 degrees drift for every hour compared to the *three degree drift in 15 minutes* on the 1937 instrument Amelia used in her *Electra*.

The autopilot instrument shown in the photo is located on a prominent position in the center portion of the instrument panel. The magnetic compass is shown mounted in the middle upper area of the instrument panel. The six control levers, shown in the lower center console below the instrument panel, are the fuel mixture control, throttles, and propeller pitch controls.

Radio Direction Finder (RDF)

The direction finder, commonly called a "DF," is an important piece of aircraft navigational equipment. A DF system depends on three fundamental parts: (1) a transmitter station to originate the signal, (2) a receiver aboard the aircraft to pick up that directionalized signal, and (3) a tracking chart for locating the sending station relative to the position of the aircraft.

The receiver aboard the aircraft requires a frequency band capable of receiving the transmitted signal from the sending station. Once the signal is received, it is plotted on the chart to locate the aircraft's position relative to the transmitting station.

The receiving range of a direction finder can be as distant as 300 miles, depending on altitude. Even at high altitude, however, the signal would be weak (S-1 strength) at 300 miles away.

The DF receiver requires an external loop antenna that can be rotated to receive signals from the transmitter. The receiver will pick up the loudest signal when the antenna is at right-angles to the sending station. The faintest signal, or "null," comes in when it is pointed along the line of the radio signal sent by the station. The null provides one of two choices for the correct bearing. If the DF has a null meter, the null can be determined visually by watching the needle drop to a minimum reading.

To use the DF correctly, the receiver must be tuned to the proper frequency and the station must also be transmitting steadily. Results depend chiefly on the operator's skill and the aircraft on which the DF is being used. In 1937, DF loop antennas were installed on an aircraft's exterior in a *fixed* position. The pilot was forced to turn the aircraft to obtain a null bearing and find the direction of the transmitting station.

After you picked up a null signal on the antenna and radio, you still had to solve the 180-degree ambiguity. When you received the null, you then had to determine whether the transmitting signal was coming from one direction or 180 degrees in the opposite direction. If the pilot was absolutely sure of the correct direction to the transmitting station, from previous navigation in a particular area, then it was not necessary to solve the 180-degree ambiguity problem. You just flew toward the station sending the signal.

Modern aircraft antennas rotate so you no longer have to turn the aircraft to pick up a correct transmitting signal. The current method of using a DF is with a movable compass ring or loop by which the course steering may be set into the instrument and the bearing read directly.

Generally, when using the DF you should allow at least a two-degree plus-or-minus error, since radio waves typically do not travel in a straight line.

Unfortunately, Amelia was apparently led to believe that this new experimental radio direction finder would enable her to perform all the critical radio navigation required. However, on the majority of legs of her long flight, very few stations were available to use the DF equipment within her DF range. *Lack of experience and over-confidence in this piece of navigation equipment caused serious problems for Amelia Earhart and Fred Noonan.*

When Amelia's *Electra* was furnished with the recently-developed loop antenna for her radio, it was nonrotatable. To find the null or "no-signal" point, her plane would have to be flown in a continuous circle. As previously mentioned, the null was required in order to determine the correct direction of the transmitter.

This circling procedure used extra time and consumed extra fuel. If extreme weather conditions prevailed between the base transmitter and the aircraft's DF, the radio signal strength could be either weak or broken. Its reliability could be reduced to where the pilot monitoring the signal could easily become confused and unsure of the signal direction or the null.

With any new piece of equipment, as was the case with Amelia's DF, proficiency can only be accomplished with continuous use and hands-on operation. As previously stated, we believe that Amelia either lacked proficiency in using the DF or had not taken the time to understand its correct operation. In either case, she would have mismanaged this equipment, contributing to additional navigation errors on the long flight leg to Howland Island.

Fig. 2-8. Amelia's "Flying Laboratory," a Lockheed *Electra 10E,* was funded by Purdue University. George Putnam is at far left; Amelia, center; and the University's President Elliott is at far right, on this early visit to the university's airport. Courtesy Purdue University.

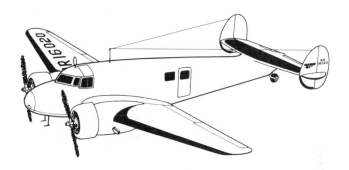

Chapter Three

AMELIA'S FIRST WORLD FLIGHT ATTEMPT

A Shiny New Airplane And An Aborted Takeoff

Trouble Was Starting To Brew

Amelia Earhart planned carefully for her world flight. She would fly near the equator from East-to-West, a distance of approximately 28,000 miles, with many refueling stops along the way. Even with a tailwind, the most difficult and longest leg would be from Hawaii-to-*Howland Island* in the Pacific Ocean. Navigation to, and refueling on, *Howland Island* would be extremely difficult. It is only a half mile wide and two miles long, and out in "the middle of nowhere"!

For this extraordinarily long and expectedly arduous flight, Amelia chose the new twin-tailed, twin-engine Lockheed *Electra*, equipped with two 550 HP Pratt and Whitney *Wasp* engines. It was also fitted with the new Hamilton Standard constant speed propellers, a Sperry Gyro automatic pilot, and the newly-developed fixed radio directional finder or DF. Unfortunately, this new equipment proved to be much more challenging to manage than that of her previous single-engine aircraft.

On the morning of March 17, 1937, Amelia took off from Oakland, California in her four-person Lockheed *Electra*. The

Fig. 3-1. Amelia's shiny new airplane, the Lockheed *Electra*10E. Courtesy Purdue University.

crew consisted of Paul Mantz, technical advisor, along with navigators Harry Manning and Fred Noonan. Mantz also acted as relief pilot for this first leg of the trip. The takeoff

Fig. 3-2. (Left to right) Amelia Earhart's husband, George Putnam; Amelia Earhart; Harry Manning, primary navigator for Amelia's first world flight attempt; mechanic Bo McKneely; at the Union Air Terminal, Los Angeles, California. National Archives photo.

went smoothly. With about six hours remaining on this first world flight leg, Paul Mantz took over flying the *Electra* when the right propeller developed trouble.

Mantz apparently had agreed to assist Amelia only as far as Hawaii. He was not aboard the plane when it "groundlooped" as Amelia attempted to takeoff from Luke Field, Hawaii, two days later.

The Groundloop Accident at Luke Field

The following Army Air Corps military report **(National Archives, Record Group 395)** covering the arrival and subsequent crash of Amelia Earhart and her flight crew during her takeoff from Hawaii will, for the first time, reveal relevant facts never before made available in a published book.

Fig. 3-3. Amelia Earhart's Lockheed *Electra* NR-16020 parked at Wheeler Field, Hawaii prior to her ill-fated first world flight attempt. National Archives photo.

HEADQUARTERS HAWAIIAN DEPARTMENT AIR OFFICE
and
HEADQUARTERS 18th. WING

PROCEEDINGS OF A BOARD OF OFFICERS APPOINTED TO INVESTIGATE AND REPORT UPON THE CRASH OF MISS AMELIA EARHART'S PLANE NR-16020 AT LUKE FIELD, OAHU, AT 5:50 A.M. MARCH 20, 1937, AND CIRCUMSTANCES RELATING TO HER ARRIVAL AND STAY AT WHEELER AND LUKE FIELDS, MARCH 18 TO 20, 1937.

PERSONNEL FOR THE BOARD

Major PHILLIPS MELVILLE, Air Corps, President (Luke Field)
1st Lieut. KENNETH A. ROGERS, Air Corps, Member (Wheeler Field)
1st Lieut. HARRY S. BISHOP, Air Corps, Member (Luke Field)
2nd Lieut. NORMAN L. CALLISH, Air-Reserve, Recorder (Luke Field)

This Board comprises the standing ACCIDENT CLASSIFI-CATION COMMITTEE, LUKE FIELD, T.H. (A.C. Circular 15-14, 3/1/34) with the addition of one member from WHEELER FIELD appointed per oral order of the Commanding General, 18th Composite Wing.

Oral instructions to the Board were to investigate and render a detailed, *confidential* (authors' italics) report on the circumstances of the crash of Miss Earhart's Lockheed *Electra* airplane at Luke Field on the morning of March 20, 1937, including, for the record, an account of the preparations made for her arrival at Wheeler Field; her stay at that post; the transfer of her airplane to Luke Field; preparations for her take-off for Howland Island and a detailed report of all services rendered by the personnel of either post and the Hawaiian Air Depot, from the date of arrival until the airplane was shipped aboard the S.S. LURLINE, March 27, 1937.

The Board was convened at Luke Field in accordance with the foregoing instructions at 8:30 a.m. March 22, 1937.

Present: All Members.

At this meeting the instructions to the board were imparted to all members; arrangements made for the collection of signed statements from competent eyewitnesses; the Wheeler Field member was instructed to secure a statement covering the details of Miss Earhart's arrival and stay at the post; Headquarters Luke Field, were called upon for a similar report; the Commanding Officer, Hawaiian Air Depot was called upon for a report of the facilities placed at Miss Earhart's disposal and services rendered by Depot personnel; disposition of the wrecked airplane; inventory of equipment, etc. Members of the Board who had not previously done so then inspected the Luke Field landing mat, the wheel tracks of Miss Earhart's airplane and the damaged airplane in the Final Assembly Hangar, Hawaiian Air Depot.

The Board was adjourned, subject to call, at 11:30 A.M. same date.

The Board was reconvened at the call of the President at 8:30 A.M. March 24, 1937, to review the evidence then available.

Present: All members.

The Board was adjourned at 10:00 A.M. same date, pending completion of these proceedings.

Due to the fact that Miss Earhart and her party left Honolulu aboard the S.S. MALOLO at Noon, March 20, 1937, the Board was unable to obtain any statements from the personnel involved in the crash and has had recourse to Miss Earhart's statements to the Press as published in Honolulu newspapers.

After due consideration of the available evidence the Board reconstructs the details and sequence of events from the time of Miss Earhart's arrival on the morning of March 18 to her departure at Noon, March 20, 1937 substantially as follows:

In the following Wheeler Field portion of the military report, the first factual evidence concerning Earhart's propeller problems enroute to Hawaii is presented from **National Archives, Record Group 395:**

WHEELER FIELD:

Miss Amelia Earhart with Mr. Paul Mantz, technical advisor, Captain Harry Manning, navigator and Mr. Fred J. Noonan, co-pilot and assistant navigator, landed in her Lockheed *Electra* airplane, Department of Commerce No. NR 16020 at Wheeler Field, T.H. at 5:45 A.M. March 18, 1937, having flown from Oakland, California on the first leg of a projected "Round-the-World-Flight." Comprehensive preparations for her arrival previously made by the Commanding Officer, Wheeler Field were put into immediate effect.

The airplane was placed under cover in the hangar of the 75th Service Squadron and the personnel of the flight, after breakfasting at the quarters of the Commanding Officer, Wheeler Field, left for rest at the residence of Mr. Christian R. Holmes, Honolulu. No instructions were left by Miss Earhart or Mr. Mantz at this time relative to the care and maintenance of the airplane. At the direction of 1st Lieutenant Kenneth A. Rogers, Station Engineering Officer, Wheeler Field and under the supervision of Mr. Wilbur Thomas, Honolulu representative of the Pratt & Whitney Aircraft Company and 1st Lieut. Donald D. Arnold, Engineering Officer, Hawaiian Air Depot, the personnel of the Station Engineering Department undertook a routine inspection and servicing of the airplane and engines. *Mr. Mantz had stated on arrival, that for the last six hours of the flight the right-hand Hamilton constant speed propeller had frozen in a position of fixed pitch.* Special attention was, therefore, paid to *filling the propellers with fresh lubricant* (authors' italics). At about 3:00 P.M., Mr. Mantz returned to Wheeler Field and the airplane was placed on the flying line for a test. The self-adjusting pitch mechanism of the right-hand propeller still failed to function. The engines were stopped and the defective propeller removed for disassembly and inspection.

The latter revealed a badly galled condition and that the blades were frozen in the hub due to improper or insufficient lubrication. As the necessary tools for dismounting the propeller and remedying this condition were not available at Wheeler Field, the left hand propeller was also removed from the airplane and both propellers taken to the propeller section Hawaiian Air Depot, Luke Field for reconditioning. The Depot personnel worked throughout the night on the propellers which were returned to Wheeler Field at 2:00 A.M. March 19, and re-installed on the airplane. At this time the hour of Miss Earhart's departure for Howland Island was still undetermined but it was generally understood that she would take-off late in the afternoon of March 19, weather permitting. Mr. Mantz arrived from the city at 11:00 A.M. and was advised of the work that had been performed on the airplane and the propellers. He requested that the airplane be partially serviced with gasoline and adjustment made on the right-hand oleo leg. (Authors' Note: Oleo legs are similar to shock absorbers on an automobile.) This was done. The airplane was then placed on the flying line for engine test. During this test the propellers functioned perfectly. At about 11:15 A.M. Mr. Mantz with Mr. Christian R. Holmes and Miss Terry Mines as passengers took off for a test flight. Previous to the take-off he announced that he would land at Luke Field to have the airplane instruments checked at the Depot and if the landing mat at that station afforded better conditions for Miss Earhart's take-off, that he would remain there.

As this military report made reference to both Exhibits A & E, portions of these Exhibits are presented in sequence of importance to show the actual problems and services performed on the two propellers of Amelia's Lockheed *Electra* after arriving in Hawaii on this first world flight attempt.

From National Archives, Record Group 395:

EXHIBIT "A"

When the plane arrived Mr. Mantz said that something had gone wrong with one of the propellers to the extent that the pitch could not be changed and that he had flown the airplane for the last seven or eight hours with the propellers in this condition. From the amount of grease pumped into the propeller hubs, it was clearly evident that these hubs had left Oakland with very little grease in them.

It took all morning and until three in the afternoon to finish the above checking, but the ship was ready to be run up to find out if the grease which was forced into the hubs had cleared up the propeller trouble. Mr. Mantz very opportunely showed up at this time and proceeded to run the motors up. The controlling mechanism on the left propeller worked *but the pitch on the right one would not change even the slightest degree* (authors' italics). During this run up it was also determined that the reason the generator had failed to show a charge during the latter part of the trip was due entirely to the fact that the fuse was blown out and not to the control box being out of order, as Mr. Mantz had indicated on landing.

The ship was pushed back into the hangar and the right propeller removed and taken to the propeller room for check. It was partly disassembled and *found to be very badly galled and the blades frozen solidly in the hub* (authors' italics). This was believed to have been caused by the lack of and use of improper lubricant: an opinion expressed by both Mr. Thomas and Master Sergeant Biando, the latter the best propeller man at Wheeler Field. The theory that the hubs were nearly dry when the plane left the mainland was further augmented, it previously having been noted that there was no possibility of the grease having leaked or been thrown out since the propellers and the engines presented a remarkably clean and grease-free appearance when work was first started. At this point it was thought that Wheeler Field did not possess the proper tools to complete the work required on the propellers, and upon the advice of the Depot Engineering Officer, the left propeller was taken off the engine and both sent to the Depot for overhaul.

The propellers were returned to Wheeler Field about two o'clock in the morning and were installed by the crew which the Engineering Officer kept in the hangar for that purpose after being told by telephone by Mr. Mantz at seven o'clock that night that there was a possibility Miss Earhart would want to leave around eight or nine in the morning. When the installation had been completed and the cowlings safetied and checked, the crew retired for a much needed three hours sleep.

The crew and the Engineering Officer were back on the alert at seven in the morning but found they could have used the time for sleep to advantage when none of the Earhart party arrived until nearly eleven o'clock.

Mr. Mantz at this time requested that the gasoline which he had wanted pumped for the right wing tank into the left should be pumped back into the right wing tank. This was done and the ship rolled out of the hangar. Mr. Mantz was at this time told of everything which had been done to the plane and he said that was all there was to be done except servicing. The crew assisted the Standard Oil man in servicing with gasoline, though the amount was told only to the Company man by Mr. Mantz.

Mr. Mantz wanted some air let out of the right oleo strut so that it would come down to the level of the left. This was done under his supervision and when completed left both struts with only about two inches clearance instead of four inches which the right leg had when the plane had first landed.

The plane was run up by Mr. Mantz and it was found that the propellers worked perfectly.

Mr. Mantz, Mr. Holmes and Mrs. Miner, then climbed into the plane and Mr. Mantz took off on a test flight, leaving the instructions that if he did not return it would be known that the plane would be kept at Luke Field and would not return to Wheeler Field prior to takeoff contemplated the next morning. At two o'clock in the afternoon the Engineering Officer called Luke Field and verified the rumor that the plane had landed at noon and decided to remain at Luke Field.

Signed
K.A. Rogers
1st Lieut. A.C.
Station Engineering Officer

EXHIBIT "E"

HAWAIIAN AIR DEPOT
Luke Field, T.H.
March 25, 1937

STATEMENT OF FIRST LIEUTENANT DONALD D. ARNOLD, AIR CORPS, Engineering Officer, Hawaiian Air Depot, Luke Field, T.H.

Inasmuch as the 75th Service Squadron mechanics had the situation in hand, Major Frierson notified me that the service of the Depot would not be required from present indications. Mr. Mantz contacted Mr. Thomas, Pratt & Whitney Representative, and explained the check-over he wanted made on the S3H1 type engines. Mr. Mantz requested thirty-six new spark plugs from the Wheeler Field Station Supply, but it developed that the Air Corps could furnish only reconditioned plugs, as the supply of new plugs had long since been exhausted. Mr. Mantz and Mr. Thomas decided that the plugs did not require replacing, and the thirty-six Air Corps plugs were returned to stock.

I remained available at Wheeler Field and watched the progress of the maintenance work on the airplane during the day, but did not engage in any operation. The Wheeler Field mechanics removed the right propeller from the airplane and attempted to disassemble it, under the orders of the Station Engineering Officer. At 2:40 P.M. I was asked by Mr. Mantz to take both propellers to the Depot as Wheeler Field lacked special tools to complete the disassembly. Mr. Mantz was reluctant in asking for services so late in the day and I assured him that we were willingly at his disposal. He did not accompany me to the Depot but returned to Honolulu for a much needed rest. However, before he left I explained that whereas the Depot facilities were at his disposal, we could do no work on his airplane without specific instructions from him and requested his supervision where possible.

The Commanding Officer of the Depot was notified and the following qualified employees were assigned to the propeller job:

H.C. Miller, Superintendent	H.L. Roberson, Mechanic
H.G. Owens, Inspector	Cpl. E.J. Cashman, Assistant
H.L. Heidlebaugh, Foreman	Pvt. T.A. Dybicz, Assistant

The propellers arrived at the Depot at 4:00 P.M. March 18, 1937, and were returned to Wheeler Field via their own transportation on the 12:45 A.M. Ferry Boat the following morning. These employees worked continuously on the job and I obtained sandwiches and coffee through the courtesy of the 65th Service Squadron Mess. Colonel Harmon, Major Bradshaw, and Mr. Thomas visited the Depot at 8:00 P.M. I kept Mr. Mantz frequently informed by telephone of the progress.

The blades on the right-hand propeller were found to be frozen solidly to the hub approximately half way between high and low pitch, and it was necessary to use hot kerosene to accomplish disassembly. The bearing surface was found slightly galled which was removed by hand honing. The hub was found lubricated with a soft-putty-like compound which, according to consensus of opinion, was much thicker than our Air Corps Specification Grease. It may have been the icing encountered on the flight by Mr. Mantz that rendered this compound useless as a lubricant, thereby causing the blades to bind in the hub. On this type propeller the blades have a certain freedom of movement between low and high pitch positions. Inasmuch as it was desired to reassemble this propeller at the designed pitch, I contacted Mr. Mantz for information, but he did not have this information about the pitch angle. He ordered that the maximum pitch be made to correspond with the left-hand propeller which we had not yet disassembled. This was found to be twenty-six degrees and that setting was made. We then overhauled the left-hand propeller and found that slight galling had occurred. Both propellers were cleaned and lubricated with Mobile No. 2 lubricant which is Air Corps Specification for summer use.

I went to Wheeler Field on the morning of March 19, 1937 and explained thoroughly to Mr. Mantz the exact procedure on the propellers at the Depot and he agreed to give me a report after his test flight. At noon Mr. Mantz, Mr. Chris Holmes, and Miss Terry Minor made a normal take-off from Wheeler Field and the following crew was assigned to Mr. Mantz.

> Fred Wood, Chief Inspector, in charge
> Geo. Miller
> A.L. Sanderson
> L. Lewis
> L. Fry
> E.L. Heidlebaugh
> H.R. Beacon
> L.V. Young

Mr. Mantz reported to me that the propellers worked excellently and functioned better than they had ever done previously. This remark was made in the presence of General Yount.

In the early afternoon Mrs. Putnam told me that her plans were dependent upon the weather entirely. Mr. Mantz requested me to house his airplane and the following procedure was outlined by him.

1. Furnish him with a Sperry Instrument Mechanic. Mr. Gibson and Mr. Beacon were assigned, and after a brief check on the instruments they were pronounced OK by Mr. Mantz and no work was performed or was necessary.

The Preparation, Takeoff Run and Groundloop at Luke Field, Hawaii

The investigative board report **(National Archives, Record Group 395)** continues with an account of preparations for Amelia Earhart's first world flight attempt and the subsequent crash of her Lockheed *Electra* takeoff from Luke Field, Hawaii.

The Operations Officer at Luke Field was notified by telephone of Mr. Mantz's intention prior to his departure from Wheeler Field and steps were immediately taken to clear the airdrome. Mr. Mantz landed safely at about 12:00 Noon. The landing was reported by telephone to the Operations Officer, 18th Composite Wing, Fort Shafter. He was met by Brigadier General Barton Yount, Air Corps, Colonel Millard F. Harmon, Post Commander and Lieutenant Arnold, Depot Engineering Officer. Mr. Mantz stated at this time that the airplane engines and propellers were functioning excellently and that Miss Earhart would definitely make her takeoff from Luke Field at an hour to be determined after study of expected weather reports. After making arrangements for the refueling of the airplane by the Standard Oil Company, Honolulu, Mr. Mantz left for the city at 1:30 PM

The only visitors were one or two press representatives. At 3:45 AM the airplane was placed on the apron, the area roped off and a heavy guard established. Traffic to the Fleet Air Base was halted, except for Navy personnel. Miss Earhart and party reached Luke Field via the Fleet Air Base at 4:30 AM. On arrival Mr. Mantz requested 75 additional gallons of gasoline which was serviced, making a total of 590 gallons of Air Corps gasoline furnished and a total load of 900 gallons according to a statement made by Miss Earhart. At 4:45 AM a number of Press representatives arrived via the Navy. Due to the fact that the Luke Field ferry does not commence operations until 6:15 AM there were no casual visitors or sightseers. At 5:00 AM Mr. Mantz thoroughly inspected the airplane, including the tires, warmed up the engines then shut them off. Miss Earhart then took her place in the pilot's cockpit and at her request the Southwest floodlights were turned on for a short period to permit her to survey the runway. She decided to delay the take-off until there was sufficient daylight to see clearly. At 5:30 Captain Manning and Mr. Noonan boarded the airplane and Miss Earhart started the motors. At 5:40 she taxied slowly to the Northeast end of the runway accompanied by the Luke Field fire truck (also termed the crash truck). Members of the work detail of the Hawaiian Air Depot stationed themselves at intervals along the West side of the runway. A special guard of enlisted men had previously been stationed at 200 feet intervals between the hangar line and the runway for the dual purpose of keeping the mat clear and to check the point at which the airplane left the ground. As Miss Earhart taxied down the mat a Navy "Grumman" airplane taxied out from the Navy side and in spite of efforts by a Naval Officer to wave him down, followed her to the end of the runway and parked off the mat out of her way. Flying conditions at this time were good; ceiling about 3000 feet; wind Southerly, not exceeding 2 MPH; visibility at the surface about 3000 feet rapidly increasing with advancing daylight.

On reaching the end of the mat Miss Earhart turned and, after a brief delay, *opened both throttles. As the airplane gathered speed it swung slightly to the right. Miss Earhart corrected this tendency by throttling back on the left engine* (authors' italics). *The airplane then began to swing to the left with increasing speed, characteristic of a groundloop. It tilted outward, right wing low and for 50 or 60 feet was supported on the right wheel only. The right-hand landing gear suddenly collapsed under this excessive load, followed by the left* (editor's italics). The airplane spun sharply to the left sliding on its belly and amid a shower of sparks from the mat came to rest headed about 200 degrees from its initial course. The fire truck had followed along the side of the mat during the take-off and reached the scene within a few seconds as did the observers nearest the crash. There was no fire. Miss Earhart and her crew emerged unhurt. The visible damage to the airplane was as follows: Right wing and engine nacelle severely damaged, left engine nacelle damaged on under side, right-hand rudder and end of stabilizer bent. *The engines were undamaged* (authors' italics). The oil tanks ruptured. The damaged airplane was roped off under guard as promptly as possible by the Officer-of-the-day. All unauthorized persons were cleared from the mat and the work of salvage initiated by the Depot Engineering Officer without delay. The greater part of the gasoline was first pumped from the tanks into a refueling truck. Depot personnel then commenced to disassemble the airplane, preparatory to removing it from the mat. All loose property of technical or personal nature was collected under the supervision of an officer and placed for safe keeping in a stock room at the Depot. The work of removing the damaged airplane was continued in spite of steady rains and was completed by 3:00 PM at which time the airplane was housed in the Final Assembly Hangar pending disposition. At 9:00 AM Mr. Emil Williams, Department of Commerce Inspector arrived at Luke Field for the purpose of investigating the crash. By order of the Wing Commander, he was accorded every assistance and permitted to interview and take statements from witnesses. On March 25 the Commanding Officer, Hawaiian Air Depot issued orders that the work of disassembly be continued and the airplane prepared for shipment to California. This work was completed March 26 and the airplane delivered to the representatives of the Young Brothers Company for transfer by barge to Honolulu. It was shipped, addressed to Miss Amelia Earhart, Burbank, California, aboard the S.S. Lurline, which sailed for San Francisco at Noon, March 27, 1937.

FINDINGS

The Board finds that Miss Amelia Earhart with Mr. Paul Mantz, technical advisor, Captain Harry Manning and Mr. Fred Noonan landed in Lockheed *Electra* airplane NR 16020 at Wheeler Field, Oahu, T.H. at 5:45 A.M. March 18, 1937; that adequate preparations had been made for her arrival by the Commanding Officer, Wheeler Field; that the personnel of the Station Engineering Department under competent supervision carried out a thorough check of the airplane and engines; that a dangerous condition of the propellers was discovered and remedied at the Hawaiian Air Depot; that subsequently the propellers functioned perfectly; that the airplane was flown to Luke Field at Noon, March 19, 1937; that at this time it was announced by Mr. Mantz, technical advisor for Miss Earhart, that she would take-off from Luke Field as the mat afforded better conditions than Wheeler Field; that during the afternoon 515 gallons of Air Corps gasoline were serviced into the airplane at the request of Mr. Mantz and on authority of Lieut. Colonel Hume Peabody, Operations Officer, 18th Composite Wing; that this was later increased to 590 gallons making a total gasoline load of 900 gallons according to statement by Miss Earhart; that at about 9:00 PM March 19, Luke Field was notified that the take-off would be made at dawn; that Miss Earhart and party reached Luke Field at 4:30 A.M. March 20, 1937, and that the airplane, including the tires, were inspected by Mr. Mantz shortly thereafter; that Miss Earhart with Captain Manning and Mr. Noonan as crew taxied out for take-off at 5:30 AM; that take-off was made from the Northeast to the Southwest; that after a run of approximately 1,200 feet the airplane crashed on the landing mat due to the collapse of the landing gear as the result of an uncontrolled groundloop; that lack of factual evidence makes it impossible to establish the reason for the groundloop; that as a result of the crash the airplane was damaged to an extent requiring major overhaul; that no injuries were suffered by Miss Earhart or her crew; that approximately 50 square feet of the Luke Field landing mat was damaged necessitating replacement; that no other damage was sustained by government or private property.

The Board finds further that every reasonable facility and service requested by Miss Earhart or her representative, Mr. Paul Mantz, was accorded by the Station Engineering Department, Wheeler Field and by the Hawaiian Air Depot; that no requests were refused, that Miss Earhart's technical advisor, Mr. Paul Mantz, landed the airplane on the mat at Luke Field about Noon, March 19, 1937, at which time he inspected it and pronounced it suitable for her takeoff for Howland Island; that her decision to use it was based on his recommendation; that the nature and condition of the Luke Field landing mat had no bearing on the causes resulting in the crash; that in a signed statement to the Press Miss Earhart stated: "The runway is excellent and every facility for safe flying available;

that subsequent to the crash, prompt and efficient action was taken by the Engineering Officer, Hawaiian Air Depot, to remove the damaged airplane from the runway and to safeguard it and the technical equipment it contained;" that it was subsequently shipped to Miss Amelia Earhart, Burbank, California, on board the S.S. Lurline sailing from Honolulu, March 27, 1937, in compliance with orders of competent authority based on written request and authorization of Miss Earhart.

CONCLUSIONS:

It is the conclusion of the Board that every reasonable assistance and facility was accorded Miss Earhart by the 18th Composite Wing to facilitate her flight and that no claim of negligence or responsibility in connection with her crash can be sustained against the personnel, equipment or facilities made available to Miss Earhart by the Commanding General, Hawaiian Department.

RECOMMENDATIONS:

None.

DEPARTMENT AIR OFFICE
18th Composite Wing Headquarters
Fort Shafter, T.H.
(Original Signatory)

Phillips Melville	Kenneth A. Rogers	Harry W. Bishop
Major, Air Corps	1st Lieutenant	1st Lieutenant
President	Air Corps Member	Air Corps Member

Norman L. Callish
2nd Lieut. Air Reserve
Recorder

APPROVED, APR. 17, 1937
Barton K. Yount
Brig. General A.C.
COMMANDING

The Groundloop, Luke Field - Another View

As a sequel to the crash report as described by the investigating board, "Exhibit E" as reported by First Lieutenant Donald D. Arnold (**National Archives, Record Group 395**) continued with selected factual evidence concerning the events prior and after the crash of Amelia Earhart on Luke Field, Hawaii on the morning of March 20, 1937.

EXHIBIT "E" (Continued)

At 3:45 AM March 20, 1937 we opened the Hangar and placed the plane on the Line. Mrs. Putnam and crew arrived about 4:30 AM. Mr. Mantz requested an additional seventy-five gallons of gasoline, making a total of 500 gallons furnished.

At 4:45 AM Press representatives arrived and established themselves in my office without advance notice. As soon as this was brought to my attention I notified these gentlemen that all telephone charges were to be reversed and positively not charged to me or to the Government. I arranged specific desks for their use and notified the Luke Field Operator of the telephones designated for Press use. At 5:00 AM Mr. Mantz thoroughly inspected the airplane, tested the engines and turned them off. The flood lights were turned on and Mrs. Putnam inspected the runway from the cockpit of the airplane. A light rain during the night had wet the runway. The lights were turned off and Mr. Noonan and Mr. Manning boarded the airplane.

Mrs. Putnam started the engines at 5:30 AM and at 5:40 taxied Northeast down the Navy side of the runway to the lower end accompanied by Mr. Young and Mr. Mantz on the ground with flashlights. After Mrs. Putnam had taxied about one-third of the way down the runway a Grumman Amphibian taxied out from the Navy Hangars and followed her airplane down the Field. I believe it parked at the far end of the Field as I did not see it take-off. One of the Naval Officers present with our group attempted to signal the airplane to stop but his efforts were unavailing. I took position on the Final Assembly ramp with Mr. Chris Holmes. The tee indicated wind direction exactly on the center line of the runway from the direction of Barbers Point. A very slight intermittent breeze was blowing, possibly not more than one mile per hour. The buildings and various objects were distinguishable in the grey dawn but there was insufficient light to permit photography without flashlights. The sky toward

Honolulu was dark and Koolau Range was barely discernible against the background of dark clouds. Off Barbers Point, however, the sky was surprisingly bright with good visibility. Smoke from two dredges at the mouth of Pearl Harbor was plainly noticeable. A scattered broken ceiling was perhaps 3,000 feet.

General Yount assured himself that the crash truck and ambulance were placed on alert. Mrs. Putnam made a 180 degree left turn at the far end of the runway and momentarily halted the airplane on the center line of the runway. The air being still, there was but the usual lag in sound travel and as soon as the airplane moved forward I heard the steady synchronous roar characteristic of full throttle application. The airplane seemed to assume the normal initial attitude for the take-off and slowly gained speed. Before the airplane had reached the halfway mark of the Field the right wing seemed to drop slightly lower than the left and the airplane made a slow even forty-five degree turn to the left. Half way between the center of the runway and the Navy side I saw a long streak of flying sparks under the airplane, followed instantly by the sound of grinding metal. The airplane instantly dropped on its belly and slid to a stop, right-side-up, but headed in the direction from which it had come. No fire ensued. I grabbed Mr. Chris Holmes by the arm and together we sped to the scene of the crash in my car. Mrs. Putnam was standing upright in the cockpit but Mr. Noonan and Capt. Manning had not yet alighted. Mr. Holmes proceeded to assist Mrs. Putnam and the crowd formed immediately. Lieut. Colonel Harmon established a guard around the airplane. The Luke Field crash truck was at the airplane when we arrived with fire hose extended to the fuselage. None of the crew were injured. Mr. Manning slightly bruised his right arm at the elbow.

The following factual statement by Amelia Earhart shortly after her crash will indicate exactly what occurred during her takeoff from Luke Field. *Note that the wide width of her Lockheed's right tire would indicate a heavy load being exerted on that tire and not a tire letting go as explained by Amelia* (editor's italics). Lieutenant Arnold's report continues **(National Archives, Record Group 395)**:

I escorted Mrs. Putnam, Mr. Holmes, Mr. Noonan and Mr. Manning to my car down the runway while she reconstructed the accident. I made no attempt to question her and she volunteered all information. The Press had not yet interviewed her as we were alone in my car. I heard her say to the crew, "The ship functioned perfectly at the start. As it gained speed the right wing dropped down and the ship seemed to pull to the right. *I eased off the left engine and the ship started a long persistent left turn and ended up where it is now* (authors' italics). It was all over instantly. The first thing I thought of was the right oleo or the right tire letting go. The way the ship pulled it probably was a flat tire." We stopped at intervals and she examined the marks of the tires and mentioned that the right track was much wider than the left. Mr. Noonan remarked, "This is a piece of G.D. bad luck." Mrs. Putnam replied, "Yes, it is a little disappointing." Mr. Manning was non-committal. We returned to the airplane for a closer examination and the Press began firing questions from all sides. It was noticeable that most of the questions were leading questions, such as, "You ran through bunches of grass, didn't you?" Her answer to this was, "The runway was perfect. The grass had nothing to do with it. I am sure of a structural failure." She then asked me to drive her to a telephone where she could make a Trans-Pacific call to her husband. Mr. Holmes suggested we go to his house. I drove them to the Navy Boat Dock and they departed for Honolulu. Mrs. Putnam and her crew were profuse in expressing their appreciation for the cooperation of the Air Corps. The morning she arrived at Luke Field she remarked, "My goodness, none of you people have had a moment's rest!"

I immediately returned to the airplane and found that Mr. Mantz had already begun unloading equipment from the airplane. I reported to General Yount that Mantz had requested me to move the airplane to the Final Assembly Hangar and store the personal effects in the tool room of that building. I assigned the following employees, with Mr. Wood in charge, for this purpose, and he received instructions from Mr. Mantz. I obtained trucks for the use of Mr. Mantz and commandeered one of the Luke Field guards to accompany each load of luggage to the Final Assembly tool room, and all articles received were locked up.

E.L. Heidlebaugh	H.E. Hicks	R.G. Owens
L.V. Young	G. DeVelachow	E.E. Finch
Geo. Miller	M.M. Summers	Pvt. F.E. Gaines
L.D. Lewis	Cpl. E. Cashman	Pfc. F.E. Harger
A.L. Sanderson	F.O. McFall	Pvt. E.V. Kozloski
L.A. Fry	W. Holloway	F.D. Wood,
H.R. Beacon	C.F. Bay	Acting Supt.
Pvt. E.C. Schultz	W. Jurgens	E. Baker,
J. Nelson	F.A. Knos/Supply	Supply Supt.
	G.F. Brady	J. Frias

At 11:00 A.M. Major Branshaw informed me that all members of the flight had left Luke Field to sail on the Malolo at noon for the mainland and that he had obtained a release from Mrs. Putnam. The cranes available at the depot were of insufficient capacity to lift the airplane to a trailer, and through the courtesy of Commander Mullinix a large crane was obtained from the Fleet Air Base. As the Base is closed all day on Saturdays, and as the services of a qualified operator are required to operate this complicated machine, it was necessary for them to order out their civilian crane operator from his home in Honolulu. In spite of a continual tropical rain, all workmen continued steadily on the job of salvage, and at 3:00 PM all property was under lock and key and Maj. Branshaw was so notified by telephone. Before the airplane was removed from the runway 650 gallons of gasoline were pumped into the 72nd. Squadron Service Truck to lessen the weight of the airplane and reduce the fire hazard. This truck was turned over to Lieut. Bishop, Station Engineering Office, Luke Field. On March 21, 1937 Sergeant Charbaugh and I plotted the wheel marks on the runway and a chart was prepared. The permanent white center lines of the runway were used as base lines in preparing this chart, and measurements were frequently checked back on these lines. A sheet of graph paper was used and the track was plotted at five foot intervals. Due to the many automobile and airplane tracks on the runway at the turn around and beginning of take-off it was impossible to identify the Lockheed tracks, and no attempt was made to plot unidentified tracks or to locate position of actual turn around or point of take-off. Only those points easily identified were plotted. Mr. Williams, Department of Commerce Inspector, had

taken only a few measurements of the tracks, and I deemed it advisable to preserve as much information as possible. At 9:00 AM March 22, 1937, Mr. Williams arrived at my office and announced he was prepared to begin his investigation. I requested Mr. Williams to please advise General Yount of his intentions, and he did so. General Yount ordered me to render Mr. Williams such assistance as was necessary in connection with his official duties. General Yount also advised that the forming of an opinion of the accident was Mr. Williams own responsibility. Mr. Williams spent the entire day in routine investigation work on the airplane and did not discuss the accident with me. He left Luke Field at 3:00 P.M. Depot employees removed the wings from the airplane upon order of Major Branshaw but no further work was done. On March 23, 1937 the remaining 165 gallons of gasoline which could not be removed when the airplane was on the runway, was drained. This gasoline was placed in 55 gallon drums, marked with the number of the airplane, NR-16020 and the words, "Hold Until Further Notice." The drums were turned over to the Depot Supply Officer with verbal instructions as shown in quotes above. Major Branshaw notified me at 10:00 A.M. to withhold all work in connection with the airplane until further orders. However, I was to lay temporary plans to crate and prepare for shipment upon short notice. Mr. Baker of the Depot Supply already had plans laid out and material ready, including engine crates, in case the engines were removed for shipment. Mr. Williams was on duty all day and asked the following employees for statements on what they saw at the time of the accident.

Miss K.A. Haenisch	A.L. Anderson	Pvt. E.G. Schultz
Fred Wood	E.L. Heidlebaugh	H.R. Beacom
L.D. Lewis	G.H. Miller	L.A. Fry
Cpt. E.J. Cashman	L.V. Young	

On March 24, 1937 no work was accomplished on the airplane. The Air Corps Accident Board, consisting of Major Melville, Lieut. K.A. Rogers, and Lieut. H.S. Bishop, inspected the airplane. On March 25, 1937 at 9:10 A.M. Major Branshaw notified me to proceed with preparing the airplane for shipment on the Lurline. Mr. Wood and I checked the pitch angle of both propellers after they were removed from the engines and found them to be in low pitch position and identical as to setting. Both oleo leg air valves were inspected and found apparently in good order. The engines were removed and crated and all miscellaneous articles were inventoried by the Supply Section and packed for shipment. The airplane fuselage and engines were coated with a rust and corrosion preventative. Fabric covers and boots were installed over the engine nacelles and wing butts. A cradle was fitted to the fuselage as a support in place of the landing gear. Due to the short notice given on deadline for shipment, the crew worked continuously on the job until 8:00 PM. Very close supervision had been given all operations on this airplane since it was placed in the Depot's care by Mrs. Putnam, and absolutely no damage was done to the airplane or accessories while in our care. The cost Accounting Department had maintained an accurate record to time and labor on all operations in which this Depot was involved.

Depot employees were cautioned from time to time that although there was no secrecy concerning this flight, it would not be considered good policy for them to express themselves on any matter involving their personal opinion (authors' italics). All inquiries were referred to members of the crew on the flight when possible, or were referred to Major Melville.

On March 27, 1937 the process for completing the airplane for shipment was completed. Slings were adjusted and wrapped with felt padding to prevent scratching the fuselage. A thorough inspection was made of the completed job by Maj. Branshaw, and the windows and nose section compartment sealed. The cabin door was locked and all property was officially placed in the care of the Young Brothers Representative at 2:30 PM. All Depot employees cooperated whole-heartedly and willingly. In spite of long hours and adverse conditions they enjoyed it.

Signed -
Donald D. Arnold,
1st Lieutenant Air Corps
Depot Engineering Officer

Eyewitness — An Iota of Truth

The two crash reports obtained from the military records previously presented are nearly identical up to the actual takeoff roll by Amelia Earhart. Eyewitness accounts from two Luke Field civilian employees begin to touch on the true cause of the groundloop of Earhart's Lockheed *Electra* **(National Archives, Record Group 395).**

> HAWAIIAN AIR DEPOT
> Luke Field, T.H.
> March 23, 1937

Eyewitness account of crash of AMELIA EARHART'S airplane at Luke Field, T.H. Saturday, March 20, 1937.

On Friday, March 19th, Mr. Thomas, Pratt & Whitney representative asked me if I would do a little work on the engines of Miss Earhart's ship. I went over to the ship and removed the two oil strainers and cleaned them. After a good cleaning, I reinstalled them and securely safetyed them under Mr. Thomas' supervision. I then helped to refuel the ship and also cleaned the fuel strainers. The ship was then put into the hangar and the doors were closed and guards placed around the hangar.

Shortly after 4:15 AM March 20th, the ship was taken out on the line where Mr. Paul Mantz gave the engines and ship a thorough going over. The ship was then taxied down to the north end of the flying field in preparation for the take-off to Howland Island; the time was 5:50 AM.

I had walked down to about the middle of the flying field to be on hand in case of any mishap. In a few minutes the ship was turned around and headed back up the field on the take-off. *It seemed to me that the left engine was turning over a little faster than the right engine* (authors' italics) and the ship was taking its course slightly toward the right of the field where I was standing. At about one hundred yards away from me the right engine seemed to take a quick hold and the ship at once changed its course from the right to a sharp left —about a quarter circle. At this point the right wing seemed to settle toward the ground and the left wing upwards. The left wheel had left the ground and remained in that position for about fifty or sixty feet before the right running gear gave way and let the ship come down on its under-carriage. The tire gave way just as the ship settled down on its right side.

This is a true statement of what I saw of the crash from where I was standing.

Signed - George H. Miller,
Civilian Employee
HAWAIIAN AIR DEPOT

HAWAIIAN AIR DEPOT
Luke Field, T.H.
March 23, 1937

Eyewitness account of crash of AMELIA EARHART'S airplane at Luke Field, T.H. Saturday, March 20, 1937.

While stationed about midway of the runway and about thirty yards off the edge, I watched Miss Earhart's *Electra*, NR16020, attempt to take off. I noticed that when she swung around at the end of the runway to take-off *she was slightly to the right of the runway center line* (authors' italics). With the ship in this position I was on her right. About three or four minutes later she gave both engines the throttle and started to take-off. About one-third of the way down the runway I noticed the right wing begin to sag and the ship *veer slightly to the right* (authors' italics). Then, just as suddenly as the ship veered to the right, it started back to the left. After it travelled about fifty yards with the right wing very low, I heard a report similar to a tire blowing out, and a loud screeching as though it was tires. The ship continued on around to the left in a groundloop with a shower of sparks coming out from underneath its belly, and came to rest headed almost in the same direction from whence it came.

Signed - Lynn V. Young
Civilian Employee
HAWAIIAN AIR DEPOT

Amelia and the Press

The Military Crash Investigation Board did not have sufficient time to question Amelia Earhart or any of her crew after the crash. The board obtained most, if not all, of its post-crash information directly from local Hawaiian newspaper releases.

Amelia must have had her own personal reasons for not wishing to be questioned by the military, but she did not appear too annoyed to answer questions from the local press prior to her departure to California that same day.

Newspaper stories published by *The Advertiser* and the *Star Bulletin* of Hawaii contain direct answers by Amelia Earhart concerning the crash at Luke Field earlier on the morning of March 20, 1937. Verbatim copies of these news releases (courtesy of National Archives) follow in their order of importance. Note that the military investigators held to the theory that the crash was caused by the failure of the right landing gear. There is absolutely no mention of a *propeller failure.*

Amelia contends that the right shock absorber failed. Paul Mantz, Amelia Earhart's technical advisor, offered no explanation for the cause of the crash and remained strangely silent, avoiding any questioning by the local news media.

The Advertiser
AMELIA'S OWN STORY!
HOW LOCKHEED CRASHED
By Amelia Earhart
Luke Field, 7:30 A.M., March 20, 1937

It's amazing how much can happen in one dawn. Instead of being 150 miles enroute to Howland Island by airplane, the crew of the Lockheed Electra in just four hours will be taking the steamer *Malolo* back to Oakland.

The airplane which brought us here so gallantly is being dismantled by efficient Army mechanics at Luke Field for shipment back to the factory at Burbank, California. Her landing gear is wiped off and one wing is damaged. The all precious engines are not hurt nor is the body itself.

What happened?

Only one of the little incidents of aviation which are small in themselves but have serious consequences.

CAUSE UNKNOWN

Witnesses said a tire blew out. However, after studying the tracks carefully I believe that may not have been the primary cause of accident. The right shock absorber as it lengthened, may have given way.

Watchers on the ground saw the wing drop. Suddenly the plane pulled to the right. *I immediately reduced power on the left or opposite engine and succeeded in changing the swing of the plane from the right to the left* (editor's italics). For a moment I thought I would be able to gain control of the *Electra* and straighten out the course.

But alas, the load was so heavy that once we were started in the arc there was nothing to do but let the plane groundloop as easily as possible.

GASOLINE SPILLS

With the excessive weight placed on the landing gear on the right, it was wrenched free and gasoline sprayed from the drain on the right well. That there was no resulting fire is surely a result of the kind wishes and generous thoughts which have come from all over the world.

That no-one was even shaken attests to the sturdiness of construction and general safety of the aircraft.

I must say a good word for Fred Noonan and Harry Manning. They were both calm as could be. In fact, when the first men reached the plane and opened the cabin door Fred Noonan methodically began folding up his charts. He says that when I fly again, he is ready to go along.

I feel that this is only a postponement of my flight. I hope to carry out the original plans. That will mean the Honolulu-Oakland part of the Pacific for the third time.

HEAVY FUEL LOAD

I had 900 gallons of gasoline aboard. That was almost as much as I had to come here from Oakland although the contemplated distance to Howland Island is 600 miles shorter.

I was doubtful of the weather and took along enough to return after eight hours if it was necessary for any reason. However, this load was not the ship's limit by any means. So easily was the plane running down the runway that I thought the take-off was over. In ten seconds more we would have been off and would have had the landing gear up. There was no indication that anything was off normal until something happened on the right side.

In retrospect, I am thankful that the failure occurred here rather than landing on perhaps some isolated corner far from help.

SAYS THANKS TO ALL

I am particularly sorry to have any kind of a mishap on Luke Field. The runway is excellent and every facility for safe flying available. My present wish is to follow through as soon as the plane and engines are reconditioned.

May I express my thanks to all who have been standing by so faithfully and warn them that I shall ask their cooperation again? This list includes member of the U.S. Coastguard, army, and navy officials, radio men both private and governmental, mechanics around the world, fuel and oil distributors and others who promised their help in countless ways.

Star Bulletin
AMELIA CRASH MAY NEVER BE FULLY SOLVED
Army Opens Investigation
But Air Chief Doubts Complete Solution
3/22/37
Undercarriage of Plane
So Badly Damaged It
Balks Conclusions

OAKLAND, CAL. March 22 (AP) — Amelia Earhart plans a new attempt to fly around the world at the equator after her wrecked airplane is repaired, her husband, George Palmer

Putnam, said today, but does not contemplate a race against time.

Informed that he had been quoted as saying his wife would make a "speed flight," Mr. Putnam denied making such statement.

What cause or series of causes resulted in the unhappy ending of Amelia Earhart's world flight probably will remain a permanent mystery.

This was indicated today following first session of an army investigation of the crash which occurred in the gray dawn at Luke Field Saturday.

Brig. Gen. Barton K. Yount, in charge of the inquiry, said the investigation was entirely routine and exclusively for the use of the war department.

We are treating Miss Earhart's accident just as we would the crackup of an Army airplane. Our investigation is routine. Findings will be sent to the war department.

Nothing will be released for publication except at the discretion of the war department, Gen. Yount said.

Gen. Yount said it was his informal opinion the cause of the crash will never be exactly determined (authors' italics).

The under carriage of Miss Earhart's plane was so badly damaged, he said, that it is utterly impossible to determine what happened.

"Anybody's opinion, based upon what evidence we have available is not worth a whoop."

"Publication of such an opinion might result in unfavorable , acrimonious discussion which would not benefit anyone" (authors' italics).

"Only Miss Earhart's coolness prevented injury," Gen. Yount said.

"I have seen and participated in many crashes and never saw anyone come out so cooly as she" (editor's italics).

Gen. Yount stressed the fact that the army inquiry is thoroughly routine; *does not seek to place blame or responsibility on anyone* (authors' italics).

Meanwhile Miss Earhart's damaged plane is in the Luke Field hangar awaiting instructions from Miss Earhart.

Emil Williams, Department of Commerce inspector, was expecting to make a civil inquiry into the accident (authors' italics).

The Advertiser
3/22/37
ARMY SEEKS EXACT CAUSE OF CRACK-UP
Earhart Crash Inquiry to Begin Today;
Wrecked Plane Being Shipped to Lockheed Factory

While Amelia Earhart's wrecked Lockheed *Electra* "flying laboratory" lies partly dismantled at Luke Field preparatory to being made ready for shipment on the *Lurline* Saturday, Army officials will start an inquiry this morning to determine the cause behind Saturday's near tragedy.

The first step will be to study photographs of the wreckage that once was the pride of Amelia's heart and to closely question witnesses who were present at the unfortunate attempted take-off.

THEORIES EXPRESSED

Army officers, when questioned as to what they considered to be the cause of the crackup said, unofficially, they favored the opinion that the landing gear gave way before the tire blew out. They pointed out that new tires had been installed and were checked carefully just three minutes before take-off.

They also pointed out that the right tire track was wider from the point where the plane began to skid. This indicated, the officers said, that the right tire was either becoming deflated or that it was required to bear increased weight due to the starboard tilt of the plane. This tilt to the right, they said, would be due possibly to failure of the shock absorbers or other parts of the right wheel gear.

BEING SENT TO FACTORY

The damaged Lockheed *Electra* is being shipped back to the Lockheed factory in Burbank, Calif. for repairs. Amelia says she will "try again." Her husband, George Palmer Putnam, announced: "The flight will be continued. The crew will stay with her until hell freezes over."

The three men who flew with her from Oakland, Paul Mantz, technical advisor, Harry Manning, co-pilot, and F.J. Noonan, her advisor navigator, all expressed confidence in Miss Earhart and said they are ready to take off with her again on her proposed 28,000 miles around-the-world flight.

Star Bulletin
GROUNDLOOP ALONE
CAUSE OF AMELIA'S CRASH
3/22/37

Every pilot who has flown a bi-motored plane has been where Amelia was Saturday morning.

No blowouts, no soft tires, no wet spots in the runway.

Just two tremendously powerful motors, their 1,100 horsepower unleashed, leaping forward at opposite ends of an airplane wing, each straining to get past the other.

Suddenly one motor edges a tiny bit ahead of the other. The pilot sees the shift in the plane's course, applies opposite rudder, slacks off one throttle. But the wing continues to yaw. The pilot bears down hard on the rudder.

There comes a moment when the plane is fighting to swing in one direction, the pilot fighting hard to bring it back. The pilot wins, but he wins too fast. The plane comes back in a swift swing and all the rudder in the world is of no avail. The plane goes into a groundloop from which there is no returning.

This and this alone is what Hawaii's veteran pilots believe, indeed, feel certain, happened at Luke Field Saturday morning.

A groundloop is the name applied by pilots to the mishap which occurs when the plane, traveling on the ground, gets out of control and turns in a circle.

If it is traveling slowly no harm is done. If it is going fast, the plane goes over on its side.

An airplane on the ground is traveling not on four wheels, like an auto, nor even on three, but only two.

One of the most important phases of a takeoff is to keep it on a straight course until it leaves the ground.

With a bi-motored ship this increases in difficulty many fold.

JOB FOR STRONG MAN

One other factor may have been a contributing cause.

The task of turning a plane of the *Electra's* size on the ground is no small one. Consider that the ship is traveling 80 to 90 miles per hour. A wind of this force is being exerted against the tail surfaces, besides the terrific blast poured out by the propellers.

To turn the rudders against this hurricane required strength and lots of it. And Miss Earhart is no Hercules.

The only thing the veterans don't understand about her crash is that there was no fire. Gasoline of the type she was using is so highly volatile the slightest spark will set it off.

Even though gasoline was splashed all over the runway, and the metal plane sent up a shower of sparks as it went skidding along the concrete runway on its belly, nothing happened. Her number, say the pilots, just wasn't up.

The Cause of the Groundloop Revealed — Six Decades Later!

Army officials stated that they intended to first study photographs of the wreckage of Amelia Earhart's Lockheed *Electra* as part of their investigation in order to determine, if possible, the exact cause of the crash at Luke Field.

If the army had closely scrutinized the first photographs of the Lockheed *Electra* as it sat on its belly on the Luke Field runway just after the crash, they could easily have noticed that the *right-hand propeller* (Fig. 3-4.) was in the *incorrect "high-pitch" position* for takeoff; while the *left-hand propeller* (Fig. 3-5.) was in the *correct "low-pitch position.*

Why the army crash investigation team missed this very important and obvious pitch change is certainly a mystery, unless, of course, they were not familiar with the new Hamilton Standard constant speed propeller and the correct pitch setting required for takeoff.

Either way, the military crash investigation board report makes no mention of this obvious right propeller malfunction and, in fact, their findings close with "no recommendations."

Fig. 3-4. was taken moments after Amelia Earhart groundlooped her plane during the takeoff from Luke Field, Hawaii on the morning of March 20, 1937.

Fig. 3-4. The right side of the *Electra* after the groundloop. National Archives photo.

Note that the *right* propeller is clearly shown in the high pitch, low RPM position. The counterweights are fully extended and the piston is not exposed. This propeller should have been in the low-pitch, high RPM position for takeoff, as was the left propeller.

Fig. 3-5. The left side of the *Electra* after the groundloop. Paul Mantz is standing in the cockpit. Courtesy World Wide Photos, Inc.

Fig. 3-5. shows the *left* engine propeller of Amelia's Lockheed *Electra* moments after her Luke Field crash. The propeller counterweights are retracted and the propeller is in the low-pitch, high RPM position, which is correct for takeoff.

This is undeniable factual proof that at the moment of takeoff, the left engine and propeller would have been turning over faster and producing more power than the right engine. This difference in pulling power would swing the aircraft toward the right and when Amelia reduced power on the left engine in order to correct for the swing, she went into an uncontrollable left groundloop. Both landing gears collapsed from the heavy side loads.

Following are our statements of facts and observations prior to and after the crash of Amelia Earhart's Lockheed *Electra* at Luke Field, Hawaii, on March 20, 1937.

DISCLOSURE

The report of Amelia Earhart's crash at Luke Field in Hawaii on the morning of March 20, 1937, was prepared and documented by a military accident board consisting entirely of United States Army Air Corps personnel.

Excerpts of this report have been previously presented in an order detailing the most revealing aspects of the accident facts. These facts, along with photographic evidence, show conclusively why this crash occurred.

The original Military Crash Investigation Report may be obtained from **National Archives, Record Group 395.**

FACTS

1. Upon arrival at Wheeler Field in Hawaii on March 18, 1937, Paul Mantz, technical advisor to Amelia Earhart on this first leg of the world flight, reported to the military reception committee at Wheeler Field that for the last six hours of the flight from California, "the right-hand Hamilton constant speed propeller had been frozen in a position of unknown fixed pitch."

Repair of the right-hand propeller at the Wheeler Field Depot repair shop revealed that the propeller was indeed frozen to the hub approximately halfway between high and low pitch. The bearing surface was badly galled and the condition corrected by hand honing, because there were no replacement parts available for the constant speed propeller at Wheeler.

2. George H. Miller, an eyewitness to the takeoff of Amelia Earhart on the morning of March 20, 1937 from Luke Field, Hawaii, stated that the "left engine was turning over faster than the right engine," and that the ship was taking a course to the right.

Moments after the crash, a photograph was taken which shows the right-hand propeller in the high-pitch, low RPM position. The correct pitch position for takeoff of the constant speed propeller is just the opposite; the low-pitch, high RPM position. Very soon thereafter, another photograph was taken showing the left-hand propeller in the correct low-pitch, high RPM position.

3. *Shortly after the crash, Amelia Earhart stated in front of four witnesses that "the ship pulled to the right as it gained speed on the takeoff roll." She went on to say that, "I eased off on the left engine and the ship started a long persistent left turn, ending up where it is now."*

Although not included in this book, several photographs are currently available showing both the left and right propellers being removed from the engines while the aircraft was sitting on its belly after the Luke Field crash.

In order to remove a Hamilton Standard constant speed propeller from a propeller shaft, a special wrench must be used to remove the retaining nut. Also, the propeller blades must first be turned by hand using another special tool that fits snugly over the airfoil shape of the blades. The blades are then turned and placed into the high-pitch position so that the special wrench can reach the propeller shaft nut. That special wrench was carried in Amelia Earhart's spare parts inventory.

Once the propellers are removed from the shafts, and there is no oil present in the pitch change cylinders, they can be turned by hand to either the high or low pitch positions. All that's necessary is to simply exert a twisting pressure on each blade. We submit this is what actually occurred after the propellers were removed.

In the "Exhibit E" report, Lieut. Donald D. Arnold, Depot Engineering Office of Luke Field, states that he and Mr. Fred Wood checked the pitch angle of both propellers after their removal from the engines. They found them to be in the low-pitch position and identical in setting. *This statement is contrary to factual photographic evidence in the accident photograph taken immediately after Amelia groundlooped her plane, the propeller counterweights of the right-hand propeller are shown fully extended.* This means, of course, that the propeller was in high-pitch when it should have been in low!

The 1937 Army Air Corps Amelia Earhart Crash Investigation Report states that the airplane, along with both propellers and personal effects, were to be taken and stored in the Final Assembly Hangar on the field. It was at this location that Lieut. Arnold, Depot Engineering Officer and civilian employee Fred Wood inspected both engine propeller blades, and not on the runway accident site! By this time, both blades of the right engine had been changed to the low-pitch position, identical to the left-hand propeller blades.

A specially designed wrench for removal of the propeller cylinder head plate and engine shaft retaining nut was part of Amelia's on-board inventory. Consequently, it was readily accessible at the accident site and was undoubtedly quickly used to remove both propellers shortly after the mishap.

The propeller wrench that Amelia carried on her aircraft is illustrated in Fig. 3-6. Normally it comes with a detachable steel leverage bar. This wrench differs in that an extension handle was welded to the wrench body; but the hole provided for the steel leverage bar can still be clearly seen.

Fig. 3-6. Propeller wrench similar to the one carried onboard Amelia's *Electra*. Gomez photo.

The wrench illustrated is in place on the cylinder plate nut of a similar constant speed propeller in the high-pitch position. Note that the counterweights are fully extended, so that after the cylinder head is removed, the wrench can reach the shaft nut in order to remove the propeller.

In the second accident photograph earlier in this chapter, Paul Mantz is standing on the wing next to Amelia Earhart at the open cockpit hatch. Without doubt, Amelia was depending on Mantz to have her *Electra* safely removed from the site and shipped back to California for repairs. Mantz was still very much in charge of NR-16020.

4. Mr. Emil Williams, a Federal Department of Commerce inspector, arrived at Luke Field two days after the crash for the sole purpose of investigating the accident involving Amelia Earhart's Lockheed *Electra*.

After a full day of intensive investigation and questioning of 11 eyewitnesses about the takeoff and crash, Williams left the field at 3:00 PM that day and never returned. He did not furnish the Luke Field Investigation Board with a copy of his findings.

Our survey and search for a copy of Mr. Williams findings and report, if any exist, proved fruitless. **The following records were examined for this missing report by Tab Lewis, Civil Reference Branch, National Archives in Washington, D.C. during December, 1989:**

a. The Department of Commerce (Record Group 40).

b. The Federal Aviation Administration and its predecessors (Record Group 237).

c. The National Transportation Safety Board, Public Inquiry Section, AD-46.

d. Coast Guard (Record Group 26).

The National Transportation Safety Board, a branch of the Department of Commerce reported that it had only two aircraft accidents reported during the year 1937, and neither of them were that of Amelia Earhart's plane crash at Luke Field, Hawaii on March 20 of that year.

Obviously, if Mr. Williams had made a report on his findings on Amelia Earhart's crash, it certainly would have revealed additional facts as to whether the accident was caused by an equipment failure, pilot error or both.

The following letters from Michael G. Knapp of the Military Reference Branch, Textual Reference Division, National Archives, Washington, D.C., and Tab Lewis, National Archives, confirm that no report by Emil Williams could be located in National Archives records.

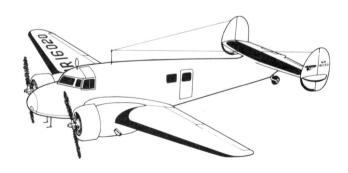

Washington, DC 20408

December 12, 1989

Walter E. Roessler
P.O. Box 3431
Sebring, FL 33871

Dear Mr. Roessler:

Thank you for your letter of November 15, 1989, concerning the Commerce Department investigation into the March 20, 1937 crash of Amelia Earhart at Luke Field, Hawaii.

We surveyed the records of the Department of Commerce (Record Group 40), the records of the Federal Aviation Administration and its predecessors (Record Group 237), and the records of the Coast Guard (Record Group 26) for the report you requested. The report is not included among the files pertaining to Earhart in any of these record groups.

We contacted the Airman (405) 680-3261 and Aircraft (405) 680-3116 Registration Branches of the Mike Monroney Aeronautical Center, mailing address P.O. Box 25082, Oklahoma City, OK 73125. This center maintains records on pilots and aircraft, from 1926-present. On your behalf, we inquired whether investigations of aircraft accidents are generally included in the files of pilots or aircraft, and they responded that such investigative reports would not be among their records.

We also contacted the National Transportation Safety Board, Public Inquiry Section, AD-46, 800 Independence Avenue, S.W., Washington, DC 20591, (202) 382-6735, on your behalf regarding this matter. Their records include investigation reports for two aircraft accidents in March, 1937. However, neither report was an investigation of the Earhart crash.

For further information, you may want to contact Ninety-Nines, Inc., Library and Archives, P.O. Box 59965, Will Rogers World Airport, Oklahoma City, OK 73159, (405) 685-7969. This is an organization that collects materials related to women in aviation.

We have forwarded a copy of your letter to our Military Reference Branch for a separate reply.

We hope this information will be of assistance to you in your research.

Sincerely,

Tab Lewis

TAB LEWIS
Civil Reference Branch

National Archives and Records Administration

Fig. 3-7. Co-author Walter Roessler's letter from the National Archives.

National Archives

Washington, DC 20408

December 26, 1989

Reply to:NNRM90-1861-MGK

Walter E. Roessler
P.O. Box 3431
Sebring, FL 33871

Dear Mr. Roessler:

This is in reply to your letter of November 15, 1989, which was referred to us by our Civil Reference Branch (NNRC), seeking further information on the crash of Amelia Earhart at Luke Field, Hawaii.

We re-checked the file: Investigation of Crash of Miss Earhart at Luke Field 3-20-37, General Correspondence, Air Officer, Hawaiian Department, Records of U.S. Army Overseas Operations and Commands, Record Group 395 and could not locate any report created by Emil Williams. As we have already provided you with a copy of this file we have not enclosed a NATF Form 72. The file does not mention if Mr. Williams provided a copy of his report to the Army authorities at Luke Field.We checked further in this series but could not locate the report in question.

Sincerely,

MICHAEL G. KNAPP
Military Reference Branch
Textual Reference Division

National Archives and Records Administration

Fig. 3-8. National Archives second letter to co-author Walter Roessler.

OBSERVATIONS

1. Paul Mantz, as technical advisor to aviatrix Amelia Earhart, should have advised (and probably did advise) and strongly recommend to Amelia and her crew that, because of the serious internal wear found inside the hub of the right-hand constant speed propeller, continuation of the world flight attempt should be put on "hold" until both propellers could be returned to the factory for proper overhaul or replacement whichever was considered necessary to assure completely safe operation over the long flight that lay ahead. A badly galled and hand-dressed propeller would have most certainly failed enroute, causing further flight delay or serious accident.

   Logic and flight safety should have dictated the need for nothing less than a Hamilton Standard propeller factory inspection, repair or replacement. The decision to render a temporary repair to the damaged propeller, a new design in 1937, indeed contributed to a takeoff malfunction and the consequent crash of Amelia Earhart's airplane.

2. George H. Miller, one of eight civilian employees stationed at Luke Field and assigned to Paul Mantz as ground help, made an important eyewitness observation of a power or pitch change when he reported that, as Amelia Earhart started her takeoff, the left engine was running noticeably faster than the right engine.

   The crash photograph reveals that the right-hand propeller was not in the correct pitch for full power takeoff. This would have caused it to lag at full throttle and sound different than the left one. With less than full pulling power from the right prop, the airplane swung slightly to the right. Amelia then attempted to correct this by reducing power on the left engine. This caused the airplane to go into a left groundloop, collapsing the right landing gear, as explained earlier. Obviously, the right-hand propeller blades had either frozen in or slipped into high-pitch during the takeoff run, since this was the position they were in shortly after the crash.

   A blocked oil passage from the propeller governor would have allowed the counterweights to put the propeller into high-pitch, even if Amelia had selected the correct low-pitch position for takeoff. Since there is no mention that the oil passages or propeller governor had been flushed and cleaned by any Depot repair shop personnel, a blocked oil passage is the most probable cause of the right-hand propeller being in the high-pitch position.

3. Amelia herself admitted reducing left engine power (RPM) when the *Electra* started swinging to the right. In simple aeronautical terms, she "jockeyed-the-throttles," (which Mantz specifically told her not to do!), aggravating the situation and resulting in the groundloop. If she had quickly reduced power on both engines, and judiciously applied brakes and rudder control, she could have given herself a good chance to avoid the groundloop. Doing that, she could have kept the heavily fuel-laden aircraft running straight and brought it to a safe stop.

   The runway at Luke Field that particular morning consisted of a steel mat surface some 3,000 feet long, which was marginal for the heavily-loaded plane. Even so, Amelia had used only about 1,200 feet before she started swinging to the right. She still had well over 1,800 feet left in which to reduce speed and come to a stop.

4. It is difficult to understand the decision, apparently made by Mantz to order removal of both props, so soon after the crash. Their removal certainly could not have made any difference in the overall weight for the heavy crane used to lift the airplane off the runway.

   However, if Mantz had quickly observed the right-hand prop's incorrect pitch, it makes sense that he wanted it removed and taken away. It also makes sense that he would want both props taken away before any knowledge-able observers could see them and report on the right prop's incorrect high-pitch. Both military and civilian personnel assigned to Paul Mantz were ordered and instructed to assist him in any way possible, no questions asked!

   Since the takeoff and subsequent crash occurred in the semi-darkness of early morning, quick removal of the propellers would probably assure the elimination of that crucial piece of crash-causing evidence. The lifting crane did not arrive on the scene until later in the day, since it was a Saturday and the regular crane operator was off duty. The military had to find a civilian crane operator at his home in Honolulu.

5. Here's another important observation, somehow omitted from the military crash report. In order to remove the propellers from their shafts, it was first necessary to place the blades in the high-pitch position by using a specially built tool. Once the blades and hub came off, two people could twist them by hand.

   Since both propellers, after removal, were found to be in low-pitch by Lieut. Arnold and Mr. Wood, it is apparent someone purposely or accidentally twisted the right-hand prop into the correct low-pitch position. This is contrary to the high-pitch it was in immediately following the crash.

6. Amelia Earhart and her crew, including Paul Mantz, were apparently not questioned by any members of the military investigation board about the actual cause of this crash because Earhart's party promptly left the scene for Honolulu and boarded the *S.S. Malolo* at noon that same day, bound for California.

7. It can only be surmised why the Department of Commerce crash investigative branch, known today as the NTSB (National Transportation Safety Board) inspector, Mr. Emil Williams, failed to file a crash report on Amelia Earhart with his central office. If he had filed such a report, why was, or is, it not available for examination?

   Disclosure of his findings might have delayed or cancelled Amelia Earhart's second world flight attempt. If the report was quashed, who ordered it and why?

CONCLUSIONS

In retrospect, we postulate that, because of the unfortunate crash of Amelia Earhart's Lockheed *Electra* and failure of the same right-hand propeller that Paul Mantz had ordered repaired at the Wheeler Field repair shop, it appears Mantz needed to eliminate that critical piece of crash evidence as soon as possible. His subsequent clearance for

Amelia Earhart to take off from Luke Field was certainly a bad decision.

Mantz surely was aware the right propeller was not in the best mechanical condition for a lengthy world flight. Even so, he opted not to have it properly repaired. He incorrectly depended on a temporary fix in lieu of a complete overhaul or exchange. He was probably pressured by time in order for Amelia's flight to continue on schedule.

We (the authors) would never have considered performing the procedure used in repairing the propellers after finding metal galling. That would have produced minute metal chips that would have circulated in the oil system of the right engine. This is especially important since the propellers were sent into low-pitch by engine oil pressure. *They automatically go into high-pitch with loss of oil pressure.*

As the technical advisor to Amelia Earhart, Paul Mantz had the direct responsibility for the mechanical safety of her aircraft. She depended upon him to make sound judgements and she most certainly agreed with his decisions, otherwise she would not have retained his services to begin with. When Mantz told Amelia her airplane was ready, she took him at his word.

Multi-Engine Takeoff Procedure

We have diligently examined all the facts thus far available concerning the crash of Amelia Earhart's Lockheed *Electra* at Luke Field, Hawaii on the morning of March 20, 1937. In order to compare current procedures and those used in Amelia Earhart's time in departing an airport in a multi-engine aircraft under similar conditions, this takeoff procedure is presented.

1. Upon reaching the aircraft parked on the flight line, the flight crew performs a "walk-around" check. They look for such things as cut tires or low tire inflation, low shock absorber struts, and damaged or inoperative control surfaces (as would be the case if control locks were not removed). They perform a visual inspection of the propellers for nicks in the blades or oil leaks in the hub seals.

Last but not least, the pilot looks for any signs of engine oil leaks. He also "dip sticks" the oil tank level and checks to be sure that fuel tank caps are secure. A good walk-around inspection of a multi-engine aircraft requires at least five-to-ten minutes, depending on the size of the aircraft.

2. Although modern aircraft are carefully checked by quali-fied maintenance personnel, the flight crew is still required to perform a walk-around inspection.

3. Once the flight crew is aboard and secured in the aircraft, all controls are properly adjusted and set for engine start. The manufacturer's approved checklist for engine start is then called out item-by-item, usually either by the pilot-in-command or the co-pilot. Each item is carefully checked.

As each engine is started, the flight crew listens for any abnormal sounds and closely observes the engine instru-ments for normal readings.

4. After completing engine start, the pilot reviews the "taxi" portion of the checklist. This entails correct operation of the brakes and a check to be certain there is clearance to move across the ramp and avoid loose gravel. Calling the control tower for taxi instructions is the last item on the taxi checklist.

Ground personnel may also assist and direct a flight crew for correct taxiing directions, especially in a con-gested ramp area.

5. Upon reaching the end of the taxiway, the aircraft is held short of the active runway and, after the brakes are set or held, a departure check is made of both engines and aircraft. This is the most critical part of the pre-takeoff review of engines and aircraft. The pilot-in-command and the co-pilot must pay particular attention to the engine and propeller performance before rolling out on to the active runway for takeoff. It is far better to detect a malfunction on the ground than experience one during takeoff.

In the case of Amelia Earhart's Lockheed *Electra* it appears that the right-hand propeller went into high-pitch during the takeoff run from Luke Field. Under procedures used today, this malfunction would be found during the pre-flight check of the propellers' pitch range prior to takeoff.

6. The next portion of the checklist would be call-out of the "before takeoff" section. During this check, both reciprocating engines, similar to those used on the Lockheed *Electra*, would have their manifold pressures brought up to the airport barometric pressure and approximately 1,700 RPM for an ignition check. Each propeller is then "exercised" to assure it is operating normally for the whole range of pitch settings. It is then placed in the low-pitch position for takeoff.

Since our analysis of the Earhart, Luke Field crash investigation focuses on a right-hand propeller problem, you may want to review the previous chapter describing the constant speed propeller.

7. After the flight crew completes the engines, propellers, instruments and aircraft checks, each control surface, i.e., the rudder, ailerons, and elevators are operated for freedom of movement. Then the flaps are run up and down their full travel range to check correct operation. A faulty flap on either side of the wing could result in the aircraft rolling over on takeoff.

When the control tower grants permission for takeoff, the co-pilot or command pilot taxis out to the center line of the active runway after completing a clearing turn to check for any aircraft that may be landing. Once the plane is lined up facing down the active runway, brakes are applied and the throttles advanced to takeoff power on both engines.

When proper engine instrument readings are obtained and the pilot also hears the proper sound from the engines, the brakes are released and the takeoff roll is started. Using the center of the runway assures the pilot of sufficient room should he suddenly be faced with a crosswind. It also provides for maneuvering room if a sudden malfunction occurs before flight is achieved.

8. As the aircraft gains speed, the flight crew observes the airspeed indicator, RPM and manifold pressure gauges. If everything continues to read in the green, the pilot will continue to hold the ship running on a straight line until takeoff speed is reached.

At this critical time, if an engine suddenly loses power or "burps," the takeoff should be aborted immediately. This can be safely accomplished if enough runway is left, by simultaneously reducing power on both engines. The aircraft must also be running as straight as possible, using both brakes and rudder, assuring a safe stop, thereby avoiding a groundloop.

At no time during the takeoff roll when an abort is required, should the pilot "jockey" the throttles as Amelia Earhart did during her takeoff from Luke Field. By her own admission, she stated, "I eased off the left engine and the ship started a long persistent left turn." (**National Archives Record Group 395.**) Once the groundloop began, there was no way to correct it. Her takeoff run ended with a badly damaged aircraft.

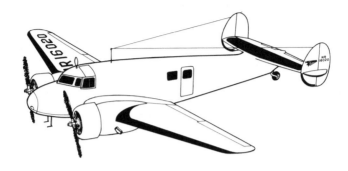

Chapter Four

THE UNKNOWN BIOLOGICAL CLOCK
Flying Through Time Zones Causes "Jet Lag"

In the 1930's, little was known about the physical or mental effects on human beings when they travel through one or more time zones. The result of these effects, now commonly known as "jet lag," had a definite bearing on the outcome of a second world flight attempt by Amelia Earhart and Fred Noonan.

In 1931, famed aviator Wiley Post, flying a Lockheed *Vega*, flew around the world in eight days, 15 hours and 51 minutes. He traveled 15,474 miles. His companion and navigator on this flight was Harold Gatty.

Their "biological clock" changes started early on this long series of flights. For example, after leaving Hanover, Germany for Berlin, Wiley Post noticed that he had forgotten to refuel for his next flight leg! He had to land, and used nearly 45 minutes on the ground while refueling. Post became increasingly fatigued and disoriented as he continued to cross time zones. His failure to refuel his aircraft was one indication that his mental capacity was becoming strained. Early newsreel pictures of Wiley Post's return to the United States after his record flight depict a very weary aviator.

By 1937, there was still very little knowledge about human sleep habits or how much rest is required for performance of given tasks. Perhaps Amelia Earhart did not question Wiley Post about his world flight fatigue effects. If she had, she may have better prepared physically to face the many time zone changes she and Fred Noonan were contemplating.

Current scientific studies indicate that the human body does not adjust to a new biological clock schedule for at least 15 days. The vulnerable "time window" of our bodies has been carefully monitored and is said to span from 1:00 AM to 6:00 AM. Research indicates that the human brain does not adapt well to rapid time changes.

Normally, if a person does not experience a biological clock change, works and lives in the same location, then no physical changes occur and the body maintains a normal work, recreation and sleep routine. For example, if an individual goes to sleep at 10:00 PM and awakes at 6:00 AM, he has slept a continuous, full eight hours and has had sufficient rest to sustain himself for the remaining 16 hours of that day.

Let us suppose that this person is obliged to awaken at 3:00 AM. His ability to function normally that entire day, especially in the later hours, will be somewhat reduced. As the body's biological clock makes earlier time demands, his routine work ability becomes impaired. He finds himself tiring earlier in the evening, and he may even want to retire before normal bedtime hours. The same holds true when later-than-normal time is applied to the body's biological clock.

The human body requires a scheduled rest period in order to normalize, otherwise physical fatigue takes over. With continuous time interruptions, it will take some time to adjust to a normal living and working routine. In a cumulative situation, the human body really never properly adjusts to the point of reaching peak performance.

We suggest that Amelia Earhart, piloting the Lockheed *Electra*, was certainly able to overcome some of these time change handicaps from experience gained from previous long distance flights; nevertheless, cumulative biological clock changes during her second world flight attempt were excessive, more than she ever experienced before, as her flight schedule indicates. In fact, as far as we could determine while researching this book, no flier before 1937, including

Wiley Post, had ever experienced as many time zone changes as Amelia while attempting to fly 28,000 miles!

To better understand the time changes encountered by Amelia Earhart and Fred Noonan on their world flight attempt, we must first understand world time zone changes. There are one-hour time changes for each time zone crossed. When traveling from west to east around the world, the hours become later as one moves in that direction.

When Amelia and crew departed from Oakland, California on her second world flight attempt in May of 1937, she lost three hours from her biological clock upon her arrival in Miami, Florida.

World time is divided into 24 zones; 12 to the west of the Prime Meridian and 12 to the east. The Prime Meridian passes through Greenwich Observatory in England. This meridian is called the Meridian of Longitude. Half way around the world from Greenwich is the International Date Line, known as the IDL. Coincidentally, it passes just west of Howland Island in the South Pacific Ocean. Amelia Earhart and Fred Noonan were searching for Howland Island when they "mysteriously" disappeared. Any traveler passing or crossing this line while moving eastward actually gains a day. As Amelia's flight progressed on this long easterly course, she was continuously adding time to her biological clock.

Her world flight, consisting of 21 actual flying days and 42 calendar days, involved 22 time zone changes. Upon arrival at Lae, New Guinea on June 30, the flyers' biological clocks were actually in an unknown time zone between Oakland, California and Lae. Although they had made some adjustment in time, they did not stay in one location long enough to start out with their biological clocks adjusted to local time.

Twenty-two hourly changes contributed to their unbalanced "sleep cycle" and their inability to function normally. Continuous time interruptions prevented them from normalizing their biological clocks. When added to a plan of a 20-hour or longer flight to tiny Howland Island, with only a day or two of rest in between, lack of biological clock adjustments and insufficient sleep likely diminished their ability to sustain their alertness over this long flight.

Some Other Famous Flyers and Their Biological Clocks

Time zone changes create a strange fatigue in body functions. For example, when famed aviator Charles Lindbergh flew solo from New York-to-Paris in 1927, he admitted falling asleep at the controls while over the North Atlantic. He nearly crashed into the water before awakening and regaining control of his aircraft. His biological clock, on his arrival in France, was running about five hours earlier than when he left New York the day before.

It may be of some interest to note that Lindbergh's Ryan airplane, the *Spirit of St. Louis*, was only a single-engine model and was not equipped with an automatic pilot as was Amelia Earhart's Lockheed *Electra*. For Charles Lindbergh, it was a "hands-on" flight all the way, but still he could not stay awake.

Famed aviator Howard Hughes accomplished a world flight the following year after Amelia Earhart's failed attempt. He flew a more advanced Lockheed model 14, fully equipped for long range flying and assisted with a crew of four. He completed the trip with an elapsed time of 91 hours, 28 minutes. Amelia's flight and world route exceeded that of Howard Hughes by far.

In 1987, Jeana Yeager and Dick Rutan completed a round-the-world, non-stop flight in their experimental *Voyager* aircraft. Although their flight totaled 216 continuous flying hours and passed through all 24 time zones, both pilots were medically briefed and prepared for the effects of "jet lag." Also, because of the design of the *Voyager*, they were able to rotate from flying to sleeping.

The *Voyager* crew was able to alleviate body fatigue with sleep, but such was not the case with Amelia Earhart. She was forced to fly for almost 21 hours without a co-pilot while undergoing a decline in alertness from lack of sleep.

When alertness diminishes as fatigue creeps in, especially true on long flights, the biological clock is constantly changing. The body becomes slower in reacting to mistakes. Micro-sleep starts to take over. Micro-sleep may last only a few seconds at a time, but when it occurs during a long flight, it can portend disaster for a flight crew.

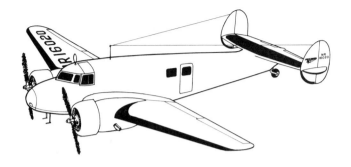

Chapter Five

OFF AT LAST

"I Have A Feeling There Is Just One
More Flight In My System..."

Undaunted, Amelia Begins Her World Flight Again

Amelia Earhart's second world flight attempt began on the morning of May 20, 1937 from Oakland, California, after extensive repairs were made on the Lockheed *Electra*. Rather than flying east-to-west, as in her first attempt, her second flight proceeded west-to-east.

The crew consisted only of Amelia Earhart and navigator Fred Noonan. For various reasons, technical advisor Paul Mantz and Captain Harry Manning, second navigator and co-pilot on Earhart's first world flight attempt earlier in the year, declined to participate in this second try. Paul Mantz did, however, schedule fuel supplies and maintenance crews at all anticipated stops along the route. He also spent many months prior to both world flight attempts working with Amelia on operation of her airplane and its newly-developed instruments.

Since Noonan would be navigating continuously, Amelia would have no relief pilot aboard. Noonan was, however, capable of flying the *Electra* during an emergency.

The flight was to cross the United States, northeastern South America, the Atlantic Ocean, Africa, parts of the Far East and, finally, the Pacific Ocean back to Oakland via

Fig. 5-1. Amelia Earhart and her husband, George Putnam, studying a chart prior to Amelia's departure on her world flight. National Archives photo.

Howland Island and Hawaii. Hopefully, the crew would return to their starting point in early July after flying 28,000 miles in approximately 42 days. (See flight route map Fig. 5-2.)

Amelia had targeted July 4 for her arrival date in Oakland. Her husband, George Putnam, had scheduled a huge reception to be made all the more dramatic for coinciding with the biggest patriotic holiday of the year. Amelia Earhart and Fred Noonan did not know that they and their Lockheed NR-16020 were starting on a "flight-of-no-return."

Amelia and her navigator encountered mechanical problems during their Oakland-to-Miami shakedown flight, and biological clock changes began the moment they headed east.

Two important factors were to plague the fliers along the way — continuously changing weather and fatigue. On most of her flight legs, Amelia had no way to tell what set of weather conditions awaited her until she actually encountered them. If the weather became too severe, she had to

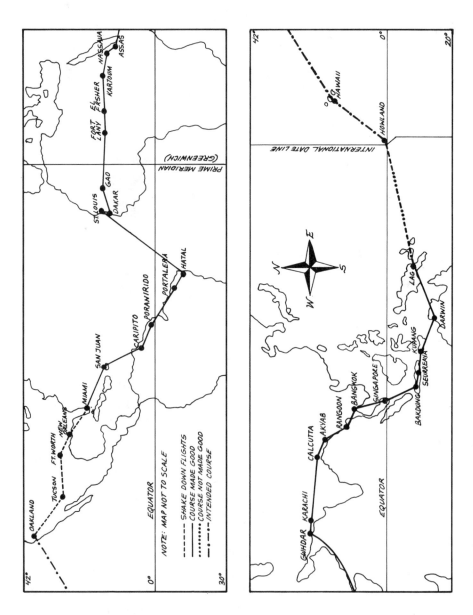

Fig. 5-2. Amelia Earhart's World Flight Route Map. The last landfall Amelia Earhart made was Lae, New Guinea; she never reached Howland Island. Gomez map.

either turn back or gamble and press-on, hoping to break out into clearing skies.

As late as the early 1950's, the best local weather reports were from other pilots flying through existing conditions. Most airlines had their own weather forecasting set up for a major part of a planned flight route; however, a good portion of the weather reporting came directly from pilots who had just flown that route! Changing, unknown weather conditions enroute surely would have built anxiety and stress. Biological clock changes would also have a pronounced effect on their physical and mental well-being, over the long haul ahead.

Physical fatigue resulting from early morning takeoffs, long flying hours under severe weather conditions and mechanical problems along the way, certainly affected the fliers' well-being. Amelia's decision to press-on with this world flight, even under these compounded pressures, would push her, her navigator and their aircraft to "the-edge-of-their-safety-envelope." Why Amelia planned her world flight during this time of year is questionable. Apparently, her planned arrival in Oakland on July 4 was considered important for promotional purposes.

Hurricane season begins on June 1 each year, extending through the West Indies to the coast of Africa, where the majority of these severe tropical storms are spawned. The Monsoon storms of both India and Indo-China are also very severe at that time of year. For instance, on June 20, 1990, a severe monsoon in Bombay, India caused the collapse of a four-story building, killing 24 people and injuring 107.

Amelia and Fred planned their daily flight arrivals for daytime since, as they traveled in an easterly direction, they were reducing their daylight hours. Many of the airfields they would use had no lights, and navigation was more difficult at night. It was paramount they complete all flight legs by sunset.

Most airfields in 1937 were poorly constructed. Water-covered and muddy fields were common. *Amelia habitually shut down her engines with the propellers in the wrong (low) pitch setting after landing, as illustrated in a previous photograph.* Overnight, open tiedowns throughout the trip would expose her aircraft to rain, dirt, high humidity and salt air with the propellers in low-pitch, the change mechanism would rust, making in-flight pitch changes more difficult, adding to Amelia's workload.

High humidity and flight through heavy rain squalls would also cause the high tension ignition system on Amelia's Wasp engines to break down, misfire and run rough at times.

Since Earhart and Noonan flew across Africa and India during the Monsoon season, they encountered strong headwinds as well as heavy rain squalls. Headwinds would have required Amelia to run her engines at a higher throttle setting in order to maintain acceptable ground speed.

Fuel fumes from leaking gasoline tanks carried in the main fuselage of her Lockheed undoubtedly caused more problems. These extra tanks were located just behind the cockpit bulkhead in the center of gravity of the airplane, as illustrated. Leaks from these tanks would have resulted in a build-up of gasoline fumes within the aircraft, causing crew nausea and affecting their physical well-being.

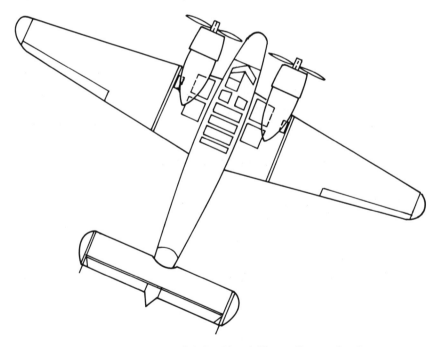

Fig. 5-3. Fuel tank locations in Amelia's Lockheed *Electra*. Gomez drawing.

During World War II, the navy's Lockheed Ventura PV-1 anti-submarine patrol aircraft frequently had internal fuselage gasoline leaks. Anyone who ever flew in this aircraft will certainly remember breathing sickening fuel fumes during flight, not to mention enduring the ever-present explosion hazard.

In Africa and Ethiopia, daytime temperatures can soar to as high as 120 degrees, making it extremely uncomfortable to touch the outer skin of a metal aircraft. Both Massawa and Assab in Ethiopia were scheduled stops on Amelia's flight. While working on aircraft, we have personally encountered such high temperatures that we had to actually carry our tools in a bucket of water in order to be able to use them comfortably. Extraordinarily high outside temperatures cause aircraft cabin temperatures to reach extremes that would greatly contribute to the fatigue factor of the flight crew. High temperatures also affect engine performance, requiring additional power for longer periods of time.

Although work was performed on Amelia's aircraft during many stops along her world flight route, we do not want our readers to receive the impression that the airplane was reconditioned, or that repairs made it "like new." Repairs were made only to the extent that, the *Electra* was "air-worthy," enabling Amelia and Fred to continue their journey.

Despite these problems and hazards, some anticipated, many unknown, Amelia Earhart and Fred Noonan were, at last, off on their world flight.

An Engine's On Fire!

Amelia's first mechanical problem occurred during a refueling stop in Tucson, Arizona on May 21. The left engine of her Lockheed caught fire when she attempted to re-start it. The engine backfired and blazed into flame. Fortunately, the Lockheed had an on-board engine fire extinguishing system and Amelia acted quickly to muffle the fire. Since no fuel leaks were reported, flooding of the carburetor on the hot engine probably caused the fire.

The next morning, they left for New Orleans, and after an overnight stay, they arrived in Miami on May 23. In order to repair the Lockheed's left engine as a result of the fire in Tucson, and to make other final checks and repairs, Amelia and Fred spent an obviously unplanned eight-day stay in Miami, increasing the time pressure on them to maintain their July 4 arrival date in Oakland.

They left Miami on the morning of June 1, flying the 1,000 miles over open ocean and landing at San Juan, Puerto Rico. They reached Caripito, Venezuela the next day and continued to Paramaribo, Dutch Guiana on June 3. During that flight, they encountered headwinds which slowed their ground-speed. Changing weather conditions taxed the Lockheed's engines during altitude changes. Rain squalls are also prevalent over the jungle areas of Dutch Guiana.

Strong headwinds would have required Amelia to run her engines at a higher throttle setting to maintain acceptable groundspeed. At this point in the flight, she was possibly beginning to experience her first mental and physical stress as pilot-in-command of this world flight.

Fig. 5-4. Amelia Earhart and Fred Noonan standing next to the Lockheed *Electra's* main cabin door and Noonan's navigation work area shortly after arriving at one of their early world flight stops. National Archives photo.

During the layover in Paramaribo, Amelia's aircraft was exposed to high humidity and, probably, rain, since the weather quickly changes and becomes unsettled in that part of the world.

After an overnight stay, they departed for Fortaleza, Brazil, flying a 1,330 mile leg over jungle and ocean. In Fortaleza, the Lockheed's engines and instruments were thoroughly inspected and checked.

The next day, June 6, they reached Natal, Brazil, where fuel was pumped into the *Electra* in preparation for the 1,900 mile South Atlantic crossing to Dakar, West Africa. This flight leg would come closest to duplicating their future 2,556 mile flight leg to Howland Island from Lae, New Guinea. To assure a daytime arrival in Africa, Fred and Amelia left Natal at 3:15 in the morning.

Amelia Had Her Own Ideas About Navigation

Amelia was depending on Fred Noonan to correctly plot their course and heading along each planned route, yet with less than an hour left in this Dakar leg, Amelia chose to fly a heading other than the one given to her by Noonan. Her decision to override Noonan's plotted course and heading indicated that, if and when she decided to make flight course changes based on her opinion, she would do so. Nearing their destination, Noonan indicated they should turn South (right), but Amelia decided to make a left turn. The flight ended on June 7 in St. Louis, Senegal, West Africa, 163 miles north of Dakar!

If their reported groundspeed of 150 MPH with a no-wind condition is considered, then it is obvious that an off-course error of a half-hour, with increasing wind speed and direction, would produce an unknown error in navigation. *Amelia later admitted that she had used poor judgment in not following Noonan's instructions.*

During the 1,900 mile flight to Africa, the Lockheed's left engine began "cutting-out" or "missing." Severe rain squalls and extreme moisture conditions unquestionably resulted in failure in the engine's high tension ignition system, causing the engines to misfire and run rough at times. This condition can, in the extreme, cause engines to stop!

Fuel fumes were constantly accumulating in the cabin and cockpit of Amelia's airplane from leaks in the fuel tanks behind the cockpit. Amelia reportedly experienced nausea on the long flight to Africa.

Amelia also indicated that her visibility was affected by oil thrown onto her windshield which could come only from propeller piston leaks. Unless corrected, this condition would result in additional problems, such as uncontrollable constant speed pitch changes, as well as low oil pressure and excessive oil loss.

Also during this leg, trouble developed on the Lockheed's fuel meter, most likely on the fuel gauge transmitter.

Amelia and Fred flew the short hop to Dakar, Senegal on June 8 and spent the next two days resting and reviewing maps and anticipated weather conditions. Apparently, repairs were made on the *Electra* during this stop.

When they left Dakar at 6:00 AM on their 1,400 mile, eight-hour flight to Gao, Mali on June 10, their biological clocks were actually running almost a full 7 hours behind their starting time from Oakland, California. As they traveled east, their daylight hours were becoming shorter, and it became even more critical that their navigation be correct so that they could land before nightfall.

Fort Lamy, Chad, French Equatorial Africa was their next overnight stop after a 1,000 mile flight from Gao on June 11. On June 12 they spent the night at El Fasher, Anglo-Egyptian Sudan. They then stopped briefly at Khartoum, Sudan and at Massawa, Ethiopia. During these flights, temperatures must have been well above 100 smoldering degrees.

On June 13, Amelia and Fred arrived at Assab, Ethiopia for a two-day rest before the long overwater flight to India.

Amelia certainly became increasingly fatigued from hot weather and insufficient sleep. Good diplomacy required that she attend receptions and dinners with local dignitaries along the route. She was intensely interested in foreign peoples and did as much sightseeing as her limited time and tight schedule permitted.

The Red and Arabian Seas passed below NR-16020 on its 1,950 mile flight from Assab to Karachi, India on June 15. Another of the ever-present mechanical problems occurred during this leg of the flight. The airplane's manual fuel mixture control jammed. Amelia could not regulate the fuel flow to the right engine, causing increased fuel consumption. In Karachi, mechanics waited to repair the airplane and its instruments. When Amelia and Fred arrived there at 7:05 PM it was early morning of the day before in Oakland, California.

They left Karachi for Calcutta on June 17 at the height of the Monsoon season, making navigation and flight extremely difficult. On this 1,390 mile leg, Amelia and Fred faced walls of drenching, dense downpours.

On June 18, they landed for an overnight stop in Akyab, Burma, intending to fly on to Rangoon the next day. Unfortunately, they were forced to turn back to Akyab by heavy Monsoon storms that forced them out to sea, flying barely above the water.

They finally arrived in Singapore on June 20 after stopping at Rangoon and Bankok. During the flight they fought blinding Monsoon rains.

From June 21 to June 27, Amelia and Fred stayed at Bandoeng, Java, Dutch East Indies. They had intended to fly to Surabaya but returned to Bandoeng because of mechanical problems shortly after departure. In Bandoeng, a crew of mechanics worked on the *Electra's* engines and navigation instruments.

While flying east, each day shortens. Amelia and Fred undoubtedly checked their flight plans to be sure their remaining scheduled stops were not so far apart as to create the possibility of landing after sunset.

A five-hour flight on June 27 brought them to Koepang, Island of Timor, Indonesia, for an overnight stop.

On June 28, they took off for Darwin, Australia. They stayed two days, apparently for some much-needed rest, since no mechanical repairs were reported. While there, they shipped their parachutes back to the U.S., to save weight.

On June 30, they arrived in Lae, New Guinea, planning to leave for Howland Island the next day. Poor weather cancelled their departure. They had come 21,000 arduous miles toward their goal. 7,000 miles of the open Pacific remained between them and a spectacular welcome celebration and world acclaim planned for them on July 4 in Oakland.

By this time, Amelia and Fred must have been nearly exhausted. The effects of biological clock changes from crossing so many time zones would have brought them to a state of desperate mental and physical fatigue.

Three days rest would have provided only a meager respite from all they had endured, but the July 4 arrival was important. Their decision to push on carried them "beyond-the-edge-of-their-safety-envelope!" The 2,556 mile leg to Howland Island would demand every vestige of skill and courage from Amelia and Fred at a time when their bodies and minds were under utmost stress.

Amelia and Fred Had to Deal With a Lot of Challenges

Before going any further, let's consider the natural and mechanical problems Amelia and Fred encountered during their 21,000 miles of flying from Oakland, California-to-Lae, New Guinea.

1. Continuous biological clock changes.
2. A left engine fire during re-start.
3. Headwinds enroute.
4. Rain squalls enroute.
5. Amelia's in-flight navigation changes, overriding Noonan's heading instructions. We have mentioned one instance. We speculate there may have been others.
6. Moisture-related engine ignition problems.
7. Fuel fumes inside the cockpit and cabin.
8. Oil leaks from both propellers while in flight.
9. Broken, inoperative fuel gauge while in flight.
10. Extremely high daytime temperatures across Africa.
11. Daily humidity changes.
12. Salt air and water exposure to the aircraft.
13. Jammed fuel mixture control in flight.
14. Flying through Monsoon storms.
15. Radio navigation failures.

This next grueling flight to Howland Island would also expose Amelia and Fred to more than 20 hours of continuous engine non-synchronization noise (the two engines not running at the same RPM, caused by improper pitch settings. Because of oil leaks in the propeller seals, their pitch would undoubtedly be changing constantly while in flight. Improper RPM and manifold pressure settings can also contribute to the non-synchronization problem, which Amelia and Fred would have experienced throughout their world flight.

Amelia's *Electra was not equipped with the automatic propeller synchronization system used on later aircraft. She had to make manual adjustments*, which some pilots have great difficulties with. Remember, Amelia had *never* flown a twin-engined aircraft before her world flight attempts, other than on short or "shakedown" hops!

Why was this world flight so much more difficult for Amelia and Fred in 1937 than it is for pilots today? For one thing, weather forecasting in 1937 was mostly non-existent. Today, we have a worldwide network of weather forecasting by radar, satellite and other sophisticated techniques, plus on-board weather radar equipment. Modern aircraft can reach altitudes above bad weather and they have the distance capability to fly around it if necessary. Ice and snow do not affect flights as adversely today because of de-icing and cleaning equipment.

Amelia's Lockheed *Electra* had a high tension ignition system. It was greatly affected by moisture, causing her engines to run rough or "miss." Modern propeller-driven airplanes have low tension ignition systems which are unaffected by moisture.

Today's pilots don't have to contend with the discomfort and danger of fuel fumes in cabins and cockpits as experienced by Amelia, Fred and other crew members flying similar aircraft of the time. Now, fuel is stored in ample wing compartments. On military aircraft, long range is achieved in-flight refueling, as provided from tankers.

Modern metallurgy provides better metals for components. Today, pitch control pistons are chrome-plated to prevent rusting. Hydromatic propellers also have dome covered pistons that protect them from the elements, thereby eliminating corrosion and oil leaks.

Equally important are highly sophisticated, automatic navigation and communication instruments on modern aircraft. This contrasts with Amelia's manually-operated radio and navigation aids.

It is wondrous that Amelia Earhart and Fred Noonan were able to complete the flight legs they did, considering the conditions they met and the equipment they used. These daring 1930's "conquerors-of-the-skies" paved the way for future pioneers and changed the world's transportation industry forever.

Now let's get back to the flight.

Talkin' With A Fishin' Pole

Strangely, Amelia had only a primitive means of communicating with her navigator above the roar of her engines. It was done by written messages sent to her by a "rigged-up" fishing pole with a clip on the end of the line. Noonan could pass notes to Amelia, and she could clip a note on the pole and pass it back to Noonan if she chose. This made rapid communication impossible.

However, the fishing pole worked pretty well. Although there was a small crawl space above the six fuselage fuel tanks it would have been time consuming and physically difficult for Noonan to crawl forward in order to relay navigation information to her.

Why the aircraft was not provided with a voice communication system, in common use at that time, is anyone's guess. Communications between Fred and Amelia were udoubtedly one-way: from him to her. *Amelia apparently used Noonan only as an advisor and made her own decisions.*

It naturally stands to reason that if Amelia dropped off to sleep, she would not have seen messages being sent up to her via the fish line. If the message contained a navigation heading change, any "sleep lapse" certainly would have allowed the aircraft to drift off course.

While still in the United States, Amelia made a decision which was to reinforce the critical importance of correct navigation. *She allowed the trailing antenna of her 500-kilocycle radio to be severed, despite Paul Mantz's repeated insistence that Amelia thoroughly learn and understand every piece of equipment aboard her Electra.* She may have found the antenna difficult to extend and retrieve, but without it, use of her radio on the 500-kilocycle frequency would be either reduced or eliminated. This frequency was the one designated and pre-arranged for communications with her support ships on the leg from Lae, New Guinea to Howland Island. *Lack of the trailing antenna would later contribute to her undoing!*

Aerial Navigation — Where Are We?

Navigation for the flight leg from Lae, New Guinea to Howland Island was critical. Any deviation from the planned flight path would result in a missed arrival time or, as fate foretold, tragedy out over the vast stretches of the South Pacific Ocean.

In order to follow the flight path Amelia and Fred took on the Lae-to-Howland Island leg, it is necessary to explain the various methods they used to navigate toward this tiny mid-Pacific island.

A definition of terms will also be helpful: *Course* is the direction to the desired destination, in this case Howland Island; *track* is the path the aircraft is making across the surface (which may or may not be the course); *heading* is the direction in which the aircraft is pointed, depending, of course, on the wind direction.

Four basic methods are used for aerial navigation:

1. *Pilotage,* a direct visual contact with objects on the ground such as railroads, houses, water towers, towns etc. These visual contacts are also listed on a pilot's sectional chart. Obviously, they could not be used over open water.
2. *Dead Reckoning* is navigating from a known position on the earth to another known position without reference to the ground using time distance measurements, wind direction and wind velocity.
3. *Radio Navigation,* in 1937 consisted of Amelia's new DF or radio loop antenna, and radio receiver bearing

strengths. An example of this would be flying toward the known location of a ground based radio that is transmitting either by voice or other type of radio signal. As the aircraft comes closer, the radio signal strength increases; flying in the opposite direction it grows weaker. The volume on the aircraft radio receiver, once set, would not be changed by the operator.

4. *Celestial Navigation* is an aerial as well as a maritime navigation method. The navigator takes angular sightings of the sun in daytime and the stars at night. The basic instruments required for this method of navigation are sextant, chronometer and up-to-date charts. The earth rotates 15 degrees every hour; thus the sightings of the sun and stars depend on the accuracy of the navigator's time piece, called a chronometer; it's the heart of celestial navigation. Equally important is clear weather, without which sun and star sights are impossible.

All four of these navigational methods were used by Amelia Earhart and Fred Noonan. *In the case of the DF loop antenna equipment, it can be only described as a failure for Amelia, for she certainly did not use it properly. Amelia's knowledge of the DF was marginal at best. Her removal of the radio trailing wire antenna early in the flight further reduced and endangered her voice communication link with ships stationed between New Guinea and Howland Island.*

It is a known fact in navigation that switching from one method of navigation to another, while in flight, is considered risky business. This especially holds true if the pilot or navigator does not follow proper procedures when the changeover is made.

Bad weather enroute to Howland reduced Noonan's celestial navigation capability, limiting his chances of taking either a sun or star fix. During one radio transmission, Amelia said "Partly cloudy."

According to newspaper reports, Noonan had failed to properly set his chronometers prior to the takeoff from Lae, unquestionably creating serious errors in his celestial navigation calculations.

With Noonan's chronometers off by an unknown time factor, Howland Island was actually in a different location from the sun than he estimated it should have been. In Amelia's last known radio transmission, she said, "We are on a line 157-337. We are running on a line north and south." Based on those degree headings, they were actually on a line running north-northwest to south-southeast and not north to south. By the compass, it figures out to be a 23-degree error in her final message!

In order to use dead reckoning navigation, you have to know where you are in order to plot to your destination. Groundspeed, wind direction and the magnetic compass heading are the three combined factors that direct the pilot and aircraft along the correct heading.

Variation. The physical North Pole is not in the same location as the magnetic North Pole, which is really located at 104 degrees west longitude and 74 degrees north latitude in the Prince Gustaf Adolf Sea located between Bathurst and Ellaf Ringness Islands in Canada. Because of these pole differences, you have to know the variation in your area between the physical and magnetic North Poles in order to establish your proper compass heading.

Deviation. This is the difference in the compass reading caused by the aircraft itself. For example, with the engines running and the radio turned on or off in flight, these electromagnetic disturbances would cause the compass readings to change.

Deviation is determined by the swinging of the aircraft compass on the ground and then checking every 30 degrees of heading against a known magnetic compass called a "compass rose." A full 360-degree swing of the aircraft is performed and the corrected compass headings for each 30 degrees is then placed on what is called a compass deviation card. It is placed in the cockpit as close as possible to the magnetic compass in full view of the pilot or co-pilot. The reason for a deviation card is to show the pilot or navigator what the compass should read for any given heading.

If Amelia's variation and deviation were off and she was flying into an unknown wind direction and strength, it is obvious her true heading was inaccurate. Furthermore, the distance both she and Noonan estimated they had already flown, would be off as well.

Without the accurate availability of dead reckoning, radio and celestial navigation, pilotage was then really all Amelia had left to rely on after her final position report transmission. Again, she needed to know what her variation and deviation were in order to accurately fly along the line of 157-337 degrees.

It is important to understand that someone using celestial navigation will at times build in a known error when plotting a course line. It is usually done to the windward side of the course, in this case the windward side of Howland Island.

When the aircraft arrives at the sun line which was previously determined by sighting or shooting the sun every 15 to 30 minutes, the navigator can then determine the groundspeed of the aircraft and will order the pilot to make a turn toward the destination point. *If any one of these navigation factors were in error, it's easy to understand why Amelia and Noonan could not locate Howland Island; it's only a tiny "dot" in a vast ocean.*

Howland Island is located approximately 1 degree north latitude and 177.5 degrees west longitude and would have required Amelia to deal with the maximum variation in order to locate so small an island. Since the true North Pole and the magnetic North Pole are in two different locations, it would have been necessary for the navigator to make a maximum variation correction to his compass heading in order to find the true heading.

Another navigational problem encountered while flying over open water is the "mirage factor." While flying in military aircraft over the ocean during air-sea rescue and anti-submarine patrol missions, we have many times observed mirages, or optical illusions, caused by cloud shadows resembling islands in the sea. Amelia was probably having a similar experience that fateful morning while searching for Howland Island.

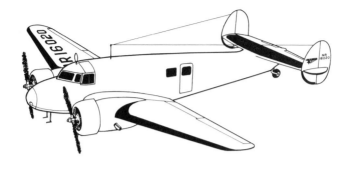

Chapter Six
PRELUDE TO DISASTER
The Odds Were Not In Amelia's Favor

Amelia's Last Takeoff

The long flight to Howland Island required demanding physical and mental tasks from Amelia Earhart and Fred Noonan, not to mention wear and tear on their already-taxed aircraft and engines.

The scheduled layover in Lae, New Guinea was only two days. After nearly 21,000 miles of steady flying, two days was only a fraction of the rest time needed before attempting the next grueling 2,556 miles and 20 or more continuous flight hours to Howland Island. Because of poor weather, Amelia and Fred waited an extra day before leaving Lae, but even so they had far too little rest.

Had Amelia been flying east-to-west as on her first world flight attempt, the leg from Hawaii to Howland Island would have come at the beginning of the schedule. Amelia and Fred would have been mentally and physically fresh and their Lockheed and its navigational equipment in much better condition.

Unfortunately, dependable weather data was not available to Amelia. *Without clear skies, and with his chronometers improperly set, Noonan's ability to navigate by celestial means would be virtually eliminated. He was unable to* obtain any type of position until early morning of the day following the takeoff from Lae, as the sun broke over the horizon.

Obviously, without her primary navigation to rely on, Amelia was, in a sense, flying blind. She was left with only her unreliable RDF, the magnetic compass, a faulty radio and a lot of dead reckoning luck to find Howland Island.

Despite these problems, Amelia and Fred left Lae, New Guinea on July 1 at 10:00 AM. Their flight would cross the International date line. To save confusion and for references purposes, we will be using the time existing on the U.S. Coast Guard ship *Itasca*. It was laying just off Howland Island to assist Fred and Amelia in landing and re-fueling their airplane.

Amelia turned her Lockheed *Electra* onto the active runway at Lae and proceeded to make a very lengthy, difficult takeoff. The airplane was super-heavy with 1,150-gallon fuel on board! The Lockheed just cleared the end of the runway, which was 50 feet above sea level, then dropped low over the water into what today is known as "ground effect." This is a "cushioning effect" that occurs whenever an aircraft is within a wingspan of the surface. It enables the airplane to carry more weight than when in normal flight.

Fuel is a Very Precious Commodity

The continuous full power required of Amelia's engines for this takeoff and climb consumed precious extra fuel. It would have otherwise extended her range, regardless of how little, which would have been most welcomed in her desperate search for Howland Island the following morning. Based on our experience with similar twin-engine aircraft, a lengthy, extended power takeoff would easily have required 15 minutes before the pilot could gradually climb-out and eventually reach a cruising altitude of 7,500 to 8,000 feet. For a 15-minute full-power takeoff and climb under abnormal conditions, based on a slow climb rate, we closely calculated that Amelia's two engines consumed an extra 32.5 gallons of fuel. This figure is based on a fuel burn rate of 65 gallons per hour per engine. They would be turning 2,250 RPM at 35.5

inches of HG (manifold pressure), using 80/87 octane fuel. The fuel mixture controls would be set in the full-rich position.

Our research on the Pratt and Whitney S3H1 engine (the same type used by Amelia) indicates that, with 1,150 gallons of fuel at takeoff, her two engines consumed 56 gallons per hour at normal cruise altitude of 8,000 feet. This would have been the highest altitude she could have flown safely and comfortably without needing oxygen for herself and Noonan.

If no headwinds prevailed throughout this long flight, we estimate that Amelia would have had sufficient fuel for 20 hours and 54 minutes and, with a steady groundspeed of 150 MPH, she could have flown 3,081 miles, or 525 miles more than required to reach Howland Island. That extra safety factor range diminished after a number of problems developed that considerably reduced fuel supply and flying distance.

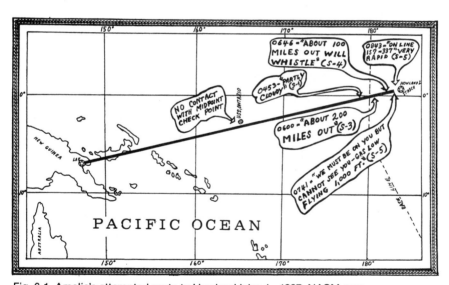

Fig. 6-1. Amelia's attempted route to Howland Island - 1937. NASM map.

Amelia was forced to continue flying at a low level until she burned off enough fuel and weight allowing her to gradually climb out. She would then take up the heading that would place her and Noonan on the desired course for Howland Island.

Why Did They Press On?

Throughout our research, we were constantly tormented by one question. Why in the world did Amelia and Fred continue the flight knowing their navigation and radio equipment was unreliable at best? Surely they realized, from previous mechanical problems, that 21,000 miles of flight was taking its inevitable toll on the *Electra*.

Were Amelia and Fred so fatigued from "jet lag" so exhausted from lack of rest, searing temperatures, and constant flying with exposure to fuel fumes, among other dangers and discomforts, that their judgment was drastically impaired? Perhaps they were anxious just to have the flight over with. Maybe they were so impatient to reach home and the welcoming throngs in Oakland that they simply ignored the clear signs of danger. Did "get-there-itis" compel them to go when good judgment would have delayed or canceled the flight? Did they ever discuss or consider not going on?

Regardless of the theories expounded by many experts, the answer to why Fred and Amelia pushed on from Lae remains as intriguing as the reasons for their disappearance!

Flying in the mid-1930's, even in commercial aviation, flight crews experienced the following hardships while engaged in long-range overwater flights: 1, Hours of boredom with the requirement that you react to any emergency immediately; 2, cruising over landless, monotonous miles-upon-miles of open ocean that caused a feeling of motionless, making navigation a nightmare; 3, using charts containing large errors; 4, celestial navigation was extremely difficult and sometimes impossible; 5, navigators had difficulty resting and sleeping was not possible; and 6, headwinds were known to cause an aircraft to fly virtually without any forward progress.

"The-Point-of-No-Return"

Midway between Lae, New Guinea and Howland Island, the U.S.S. frigate *Ontario* was stationed 1,278 miles out in the Pacific Ocean, waiting to provide Amelia with navigation and up-to-date weather information. A second ship, the U.S. Coast Guard cutter *Itasca* lay anchored just off Howland

Island to help Amelia and Fred locate the island with radio direction signals, voice communication and surface smoke.

The *Ontario* had received from the *Itasca* the report of Amelia's 10:00 AM takeoff time (12:00 Noon *Itasca*-Howland Island time). At a planned airspeed of 150 MPH, assuming no headwinds prevailed, the *Electra* would arrive over or close to the *Ontario* at about 6:52 PM local time.

During July, daylight at that location probably would have been sufficient to allow Earhart and Noonan to make visual contact with the ship. However, with prevailing winds in that latitude generally from the east during June and July, Amelia and Fred undoubtedly encountered strong, fuel-consuming headwinds that slowed their groundspeed. If so, they would have reached the *Ontario* after sundown, provided they were on course.

Before, during, and after Amelia's scheduled arrival time, the *Ontario* attempted, by every means possible, to reach her. All available reports show that no contact was made between the *Electra* and the *Ontario*. Why Amelia and Fred could not find or communicate with the *Ontario* is a matter of speculation. We might, however, envision the circumstances surrounding this failure.

Since the *Ontario* reported "no contact" with Amelia at any time, it is obvious she was either transmitting to the ship on an incorrect radio frequency or having weather and/or navigation problems. Any or all of these situations might explain why the *Ontario* never heard from them.

Amelia, Fred, or both may have fallen into "micro sleep." With the flight stretching on into twilight, two engines steadily droning at cruise power, and flight controls on autopilot, sleep may have overcome Amelia and Fred as the interminable hours crawled by. Under sleep-deprived conditions, their energy level would have been dangerously low and they would surely have battled nearly overwhelming mental fatigue.

Anyone driving an automobile over a long distance, especially at night, will readily appreciate how easily one can fall asleep under similar conditions. Today, two flight crews are aboard on many long distance flights to deal with this.

If Amelia had been napping at the controls of her *Electra*, her attention to the autopilot would have been sacrificed. In just a 15-minute period, the aircraft would have drifted off course by at least three degrees! As we previously explained, a three-degree drift angle change becomes compounded without a mid-air course correction every 15 minutes. Thus, she did not come close enough to the *Ontario* to make contact. Also, overcast weather may have developed, preventing Noonan from taking a celestial navigation fix on their position.

Amelia's radio communication range with the ship was restricted to fewer frequencies by lack of her 500 kilocycle radio. It was rendered ineffective because she had severed the trailing wire antenna!

Because the *Ontario* was their crucial halfway contact, both Amelia and Fred should have realized it was imperative they make either radio or visual contact with the ship to determine if they were on course. *Most experienced pilots would have turned around and headed back to Lae at this point.* It would be too hazardous to proceed without certain knowledge of their exact location. They would also need assurance that their radio equipment was working properly, and that they had a fuel supply adequate to allow for navigation errors or emergencies. *Not finding the Ontario was an emergency in itself!* Pressing on would further reduce the chance of either returning safely to Lae or reaching Howland on their remaining fuel.

Heedless of the significance of not finding the *Ontario* and evidently confident of her skills, Amelia continued to fly into the darkness, beyond radio and visual range of the ship. Amelia Earhart's world flight had passed "the-point-of-no-return."

The Itasca Was On Constant Alert!

Amelia Earhart's remaining hope of finding Howland Island, her scheduled re-fueling stop, depended on dead reckoning navigation and the assistance of the *Itasca*. After the *Ontario* reported "no contact" with Amelia, the *Itasca* maintained constant alert.

On Howland Island, military and civilian personnel anxiously awaited their first glimpse of the *Electra*. The

Fig. 6-2. The U.S. Coast Guard ship *Itasca*, Amelia Earhart's only communication contact at Howland Island after leaving Lae, New Guinea. National Archives photo.

following excerpt from a report entitled, "Expedition to the American Equatorial Island, " (National Archives) by an Air Corps officer, recounts how runways on Howland Island were prepared for Amelia Earhart's arrival.

<h3 style="text-align:center">TRANSCRIPT
By
Daniel A. Cooper, 1st Lieutenant, Air Corps</h3>

"The ITASCA sailed at 4:00 PM, June 16, 1937 and after an uneventful trip we sighted Howland at 9:00 PM June 23. Howland is a kidney shaped barren desert island about twenty feet high, two miles long (N&S) and half mile wide (E&W). There is no anchorage or fresh water and the island is infested with numerous large birds, rats and hermit crabs. The birds number approximately 10,000 Frigates, 6,000 Booby and 14,000 Terns. The Frigates and Boobies are the size of large buzzards while the Terns are the size of young pigeons.

The following day supplies were landed while I inspected the airport, erected the wind socks and marked off the runways with red cloth. Numerous birds were forcibly removed from the runways so that an airplane could make a reasonably safe landing."

Amelia Failed To Confirm

The *Itasca* sent a radiogram to Lae advising Amelia what radio frequency to use in communicating with the ships: *500 kilocycles*. Amelia failed to confirm, prior to takeoff, what radio frequencies she was able to use and intended to use in order to communicate with the *Ontario* and *Itasca*. The *Itasca* attempted to reach Amelia with this vital information, but she either chose not to acknowledge the message or did not receive it.

From her 10:00 AM takeoff from Lae until her first radio transmission to the *Itasca* at 3:45 the next morning, 17 hours and 45 minutes passed before anyone on radio alert and standby heard from her. What occurred during those hours can be only a matter of speculation, but Amelia's faith in her navigational skills proved to be justified; **she, in fact, reached the vicinity of the waiting ship!**

The *Itasca* radio alert watch for Amelia Earhart began at 7:00 PM on July 1. It continued straight through the night until the *Itasca* heard Amelia's last transmission at 8:43 the following morning.

The *Itasca's* radio log listed many *unanswered* transmissions to Earhart's call sign, KHAQQ. From Amelia's first radio transmission attempting to contact the ship at 2:45 AM until her last message at 8:43 AM, she was heard a total of 10 times by *Itasca* radio operators. All her transmissions were brief and at times broken by static. Erratic elapsed times between her transmissions indicate that Amelia was frantically searching her radio dial for the correct frequency for contacting the *Itasca*.

The radio log of the *Itasca* composed by CRM L. G. Bellarts, RM3/c G.E. Thompson and RM3/c W. L. Galten, shows that there were 35 unanswered radio transmissions to KHAQQ ending at 8:43 AM, July 2, 1937. We are presenting an extract of the 22 most important of these messages in their exact time frames.

Earhart answered *no* transmissions by *Itasca* on frequencies 3105, 7500, 6210 or 500 kilocycles, indicating that, although her transmitter was working, *her receiver was inoperative. She did not leave her transmitter open long enough (as instructed) for the ship to obtain a position fix on her aircraft.*

There Was Never Any Two-Way Communication!

It is critical to note the ELAPSED TIMES between transmissions to and from Amelia Earhart in the following *Itasca* radio log. These were not actual two-way transmissions. *Itasca radio operators could hear Amelia, but she could not hear them!.* The authors have inserted elapsed times between transmissions and Earhart's name before her transmissions for clarification. (Ed. Note: S-1 is a faint signal strength; S-5 is strong, indicating closeness.)

EXCERPTS FROM ITASCA RADIO LOG
National Archives Record Group 395

0345. — (Earhart) "Will listen on hour and half hour on 3105" (very faint S-1)

(15 minutes elapsed)

0400. — ITASCA to Earhart. Transmitted weather data on 3105 KC.

(30 minutes elapsed)

0430. — ITASCA to Earhart. Transmitted weather data on 3105 KC.

(23 minutes elapsed)

0453. — (Earhart) "Partly cloudy" (very faint S-1)

(7 minutes elapsed)

0500. — ITASCA to Earhart. Transmitted weather data and asked position.

(30 minutes elapsed)

0530. — ITASCA to Earhart. Transmitted weather data and asked position.

(30 minutes elapsed)

0600. — (Earhart) "About 200 miles out." (whistling, fair volume S-3)

(5 minutes elapsed)

0605. — ITASCA to Earhart. Transmitted weather data.

(25 minutes elapsed)

0630. — ITASCA to Earhart. Transmitted weather data and asked position.

(16 minutes elapsed)

0646. — (Earhart) "About 100 miles out, will whistle in mic" (good volume S-4)

(14 minutes elapsed)

0700. — ITASCA to Earhart. Transmitted weather data and maintained schedule on 500 KC for "homing."

(15 minutes elapsed)

0715. — ITASCA to Earhart. Cannot take bearing on 3105. Please send on 500 KC or do you wish to take bearing on us. No answer. Having broadcast on 500 KC resumed.

(15 minutes elapsed)

0730. — ITASCA to Earhart. Transmitted weather data and asked position. Having broadcast on 500 KC continued.

(11 minutes elapsed)

0741. — (Earhart) "We must be on you but cannot see you but gas is running low. Been unable to reach you by radio. We are flying at 1,000 feet. (very loud S-5)

(9 minutes elapsed)

0750. — (Earhart) "We are circling but cannot hear you. Go ahead on 7500 with a long count either now or on the scheduled time or half hour." (very loud and spoken very rapidly S-5)

(3 minutes elapsed)

0753. — ITASCA to Earhart on 7500 KC and 3105 KC "What is your position long count." Continuous transmission on 500 KC for homing.

(5 minutes elapsed)

0758. — (Earhart) "We received your signals but are unable to get a minimum" (on her direction finder presumably on 500 KC. Please take a bearing on us and answer on 3105 with voice." (very loud and too fast for accurate reception, S-5)

(7 minutes elapsed)

0805. — ITASCA to Earhart. Your signals received OK. It is impractical for us to take a bearing on 3105 KC on your voice. Please transmit on 500 KC and we will take a

AMELIA EARHART MISSING IN PACIFIC ★ ★ Home

Herald Chicago Examiner

RED LINE

BAN RIOT FILM IN CHICAGO

COMPLETE SPORTS

VOL. LVII—NO. 45 — — — C* — MONDAY—JULY 5—1937 — — Two Sections—Part 1—THREE CENTS

HEAR AMELIA'S FAINT CALLS

PIRATES 7, CUBS 6
SECOND GAME

(box score table — illegible)

SOX 9, BROWNS 5
SECOND GAME

(box score table — illegible)

WHITE SOX ... 0 0 4 1 0 3 1 0 0—9
BROWNS ... 0 0 0 2 0 0 0 3 0—5

AMERICAN LEAGUE
NATIONAL LEAGUE

(standings and line scores — illegible)

RUSH POLICE TO S. CHICAGO STRIKE AREA

Officials Speed Aid as Strikers Gather Near Youngstown's Plant; Post Fifty at Gates

Fifty police reserves were called to South Chicago station Sunday afternoon, as C. I. O. strikers gathered for two reported demonstrations at the plant of the Youngstown Sheet & Tube Company.

In a hall directly across from the plant gate, crowds of strikers met for an address by Joseph Germano, chairman of the Youngstown unit of the C. I. O. union.

PREPARED FOR ACTION.

Fifty police were already inside the main gate at Ninety-fourth st. and the lake, prepared to maintain order if the strikers carried out plans to protest the re-opening of the plant Saturday.

While Governor Townsend of Indiana kept the main Youngstown plant at East Chicago closed pending negotiations toward a strike settlement, the management moved in workers by boat and train Thursday at South Chicago and resumed operations.

Governor Townsend, in response to a request from the Association of Steel Employes, an independent union, which claims a larger Youngstown membership than the C. I. O., called on the Youngstown management for a declaration on its labor policy.

Marshall A. Pipin, counsel for the independent union, was assured by Thomas R. Hutson, state labor commissioner, that the union would be represented at any negotiations for a settlement.

DEMANDS PROTECTION.

Townsend, however, did not respond to a telegram from D. L. Ellinwood, secretary of the union, demanding that the plant be permitted to reopen Tuesday under protection of national guardsmen if no truce is worked out.

Hutson and the governor have been seeking an agreement such as permitted Inland Steel's 15,000 workers to go back to the plant last Thursday, but Ellinwood asserted:

"Employes insist they have been out of work long enough and demand protection of their right to work."

ANNOUNCEMENT

Los Angeles, Calif., July 3, 1937.

Editor The Herald and Examiner, Chicago, Ill.

Please stop in their tracks hostile rumors being circulated in Chicago.

The Herald and Examiner will not be consolidated with any other paper.

It will not be changed in style, character or form.

It will continue to be published as heretofore.

It is, of course, not for sale.

W. R. HEARST.

PILOT KILLED AS STUNT FAILS

CLARKSBURG, W. Va., July 4.—(A.P.)—Arch B. Nutter, 33, Clarksburg pilot, spun to his death today as a Harrison County airport before a holiday crowd of 1,000 watching a Fourth of July celebration.

Trooper J. H. Weese of the state police said Nutter was stunting for the crowd in one of a series of events on the two-day program. The trooper said Nutter put the plane into a spin directly above the airport and apparently could not straighten out in time to avoid the crash.

The cabin monoplane struck the ground behind the airport hangar.

None of the spectators was hurt.

Nutter lived for a short time after the accident, dying in a Clarksburg hospital.

Mosley's Fascists Battle 2 Foes

LONDON, July 4. — British Fascists, 10,000 strong, staged a march and demonstration in London today, precipitating riotous clashes with their radical adversaries in which several persons were injured.

Nineteen were arrested as four and mounted police fought to separate rival throngs of Fascists, Communists and Socialists engaged in one of the worst political disturbances London has witnessed for years.

Two women battled with each other so savagely that both drew blood and were taken in an ambulance to a hospital.

Britain's 40-year-old Fascist chieftain, Sir Oswald Mosley, led the march.

THE WEATHER

(weather text — illegible)

FIVE DROWNED AS BOAT SINKS

VALPARAISO, Fla., July 4.—(A.P.)—Five persons were reported drowned today when the fishing boat Nan capsized in East Pass Channel, about sixty-five miles west of Panama City, Fla.

The coast guard said a message came from the cutter Dix at Panama City, which relayed a radio message from divisional headquarters at Mobile, Ala.

Fifteen persons were reported aboard when the accident happened.

Windsors' Pastor In N. Y. Monday

NEW YORK, July 4.—(A.P.)—The Rev. Robert Anderson Jardine, who married the Duke and Duchess of Windsor in defiance of the Church of England, will arrive here tomorrow on the S. S. Queen Mary for a series of lectures.

Lindbergh Leaves to See Dr. Carrel

DINAN, France, July 4.—(I.N.S.)—Col. Charles A. Lindbergh was en route by train today to the Brittany seacoast at Saint Malo to visit the Valisine River, to visit Dr. Alexis Carrel.

Searchers' Hopes Revived by Signals; 57 Planes on Way

Speeded to Aid by Carrier; Destroyers Join Hunt

HONOLULU, July 4.—(A.P.)—Mysterious radio signals today revived waning hope for the safety of Amelia Earhart and spurred into feverish action a veritable armada of navy ships and planes mobilizing for an unparalleled search of the remote south seas.

Three agencies reported hearing the signals after Honolulu radio station KGMB broadcast instructions in the last world-girdling plane to send long dashes in series of two if down on the water, and in series of three if on land.

The coast guard also reported it heard "a man's voice or" the coming through the air about 5 p. m. Saturday, Honolulu time, 12:30 a. m. Sunday, Chicago time, and were heard frequently thereafter. The first was heard about ten minutes after the instructions were broadcast.

FAINT SIGNALS PICKED UP.

A Los Angeles radio amateur, Walter McMenamy, reported he picked up a voice repeating Miss Earhart's call letters, KHAQQ, at 4 a. m. Chicago time, and said it was too faint to tell definitely whether it was from the missing flier.

Paul Mantz, Miss Earhart's technical adviser, who was with McMenamy, said the aviatrix could have sent the radio messages only if her plane was on land, that she had no equipment for transmitting unless the right motor of the plane were turning over.

Recurrence of the signals and...

A Smile for Calcutta

AMELIA EARHART AT INDIAN AIRPORT.
Steps from plane during ill-fated 'round-the-world hop.

De Valera Holds 2-Vote Dail Lead

DUBLIN, July 4.—(A.P.)—President De Valera's Fianna Fail party had fifty-six seats to fifty-four for all other parties combined in election returns on the new Dail.

Fig. 6-3. Front page of the Chicago *Herald and Examiner*, Monday, July 5, 1937.

bearing. (The operator on Howland with emergency direction finder had heard all conversations on 3105 KC after 0600 but was unable to take any bearings due to general difficulties and unreliability of bearings on this frequency and due to the fact that *she was on the air only seven or eight seconds!)* (Authors' italics) In the meantime a continuous watch on the ship direction finder (500 KC) had been maintained but at no time was there any transmission on this frequency!

(2 minutes elapsed)

0807. — ITASCA on 3105 KC, 500 KC, 7500 KC. Go ahead on 3105 KC so that we may take a bearing on you. If it is impossible to take a bearing on 3105 KC please acknowledge. No answer. (The operator on Howland just notified the ITASCA that he was unable to get a bearing on 3105 KC

(36 minutes elapsed)

0843. — (Earhart) "We are on the line 157-337. Will repeat message. We are on the line 157-337. (very loud and too rapid for accurate reception, S-5)

(11 minutes elapsed)

0854. — ITASCA. Your signals received. Go ahead with position on 3105 KC or 500 KC. No answer.

— END ITASCA LOG —

From 0700 until her last radio transmission at 0843, Amelia's radio signal strengths were received as a five on a scale of one through five. *That radio strength indicates that she was within 40 or 50 miles of the Itasca.*

We must keep in mind when considering the *Itasca* log that their personnel had no way of knowing that Amelia's lack of a trailing antenna made use of her 500 kilocycle radio impossible.

The *Itasca* log continues:

No other reception from Earhart on this frequency 3105 KC or 500 KC although a continuous watch was maintained for several weeks. Numerous false reports were received from amateur radio operators. These were thoroughly investigated. Doubtful radio bearings on a Carrier wave by Pan American Airways at Honolulu and Wake and by direction finder on Howland were received. The point of intersection was carefully searched by the *Colorado* (near Carandolet Reef) without result. It will be noted it was later proven that the *Earhart plane could not transmit while in the water* (Authors' italics).

SUMMARY

1. There was no relief pilot, radio operator or relief navigator carried on the airplane.

2. Personal contact between airplane crew was not possible.

3. Radio operation. (Miss Earhart was radio operator and pilot.)
    (a) Earhart was not fully experienced in use of radio when used over long distances and at no time did she request technical advice from the ITASCA on radio matters.
    (b) Earhart used voice instead of key thus cutting down radio range approximately 1/3 the possible range considering the power of her set.
    (c) Earhart apparently experienced incorrect operation of her direction finder reporting that she heard ITASCA but couldn't get a null. (In all probability the null was in a direction different from which she expected and she therefore discontinued it.) She previously notified the ITASCA that her direction range was 200 KC to 1500 KC.
    (d) Earhart asked the ITASCA to take a radio bearing on her 3105 KC. She did this after being informed by radiogram prior to flight and also by radio during the flight that the ITASCA *could not* accomplish this due to lack of suitable calibrated equipment on that frequency but that the ITASCA could take bearings on 500 KC (ship's DF equipment). Earhart had previously informed the ITASCA that she could transmit on 500 KC if necessary. It is true that an airplane direction finder capable of working 3105 KC had been borrowed by the Navy just prior to sailing. This was set up on Howland mainly as a standby in case the ship's direction finder on 500 KC should go out. *However the direction finder on Howland had not been calibrated. As a result its readings could not be depended upon.* A qualified radio operator controlled this direction finder throughout the entire flight but while he could hear her, he could not get any radio bearings on 3105 KC.

This was due largely to the fact that *she left her set on for only brief periods of approximately 5-to-10 seconds. Ordinarily a set must be left on for several minutes for bearings to be taken.* Radio bearings using frequencies above 1500 KC are in general unreliable, especially in the early morning (due to "night effect") and at any distance beyond the optical path of short wave. In this case when she was flying at 1000 feet — per her message over radio — the approximate optical range would be 40 miles or less.

(e) At no time did Amelia Earhart acknowledge any of our messages or requests for her position although we were heard all over the Pacific on 3105 KC, 7500 KC and 500 KC. *Either she was unfamiliar with her radio equipment or her receiver was out.*

(f) Her signal strength was as follows:

0345	very faint	S-1
0443	faint	S-2
0600	fair	S-3
0646	good	S-4
0741	very loud	S-5
0750	very loud	S-5
0756	very loud	S-5
0853	very loud	S-5

The radio operator reported that from 0741 on, her signal strength was at a maximum and judging from her volume, she was practically over Howland. All this seems to indicate that she passed close to Howland, probably within 50 miles.

Weather conditions at Howland were:

A) Clear and Unlimited.

B) Scattered clouds with occasional local light rain.

C) Cloud conditions to the North and West of Howland would prevent seeing the island from a distance greater than 10 miles unless under the clouds or very high above them.

D) Cloud conditions to the East and South would permit seeing Howland 20 or more miles at almost any altitude.

E) The sun bore East making Howland or the smoke screen very difficult to see from the West.

The above weather reports reflect successive 90-degree compass readings from the ship.

The original radio log of the US Coast Guard cutter *Itasca* dated July 1, and 2, 1937 on Radio Log Form

2614-A revised October, 1933 by the Treasury Department, US Coast Guard, contains every radio transmission and reception between the *Itasca* and Amelia Earhart. The radio log report may be obtained from National Archives, Record Group 395, Washington, DC. In 1937, it was a court martial offense to enter false or inaccurate statements on radio logs, and that still holds true today.

The final passage from Air Corps Lieutenant Daniel A. Cooper's report affords a viewpoint from Howland Island on Amelia's last hours (**National Archives Record Group 395**):

Late in the afternoon of July 1 we received word that Amelia Earhart had taken off at 10:00 AM Lae time, that day. The ONTARIO on station midway between Lae and Howland did not hear or contact her by radio and it was not until 0345 that the ITASCA heard her on 3105 KC. I estimated her time of arrival at 0630 to 1000 with the best guess being 0730-0800. Accordingly all shore parties took station at dawn. Shore parties consisted of Mr. Black, Lt. Commander Baker of the ITASCA, Captain Neilson, myself, mechanics, photographers, newspaper men, land crash detail from the ITASCA armed with fire extinguishers etc., and a surf detail. Off shore the ITASCA furnished a smoke screen. When Amelia Earhart failed to arrive by 0900 all hands except a radio operator and several colonists returned to the ship and at 1000 started out in search to the North of the Island.

Study of the attached extract from the radio log and remarks in the summary indicated that the most probable area to search was to the North and accordingly we searched this area covering a strip 14 miles wide as we went. *Since Amelia Earhart at no time had given us her position and the Pacific Ocean being very large, the search was just about hopeless* (editor's italics). A Navy flying boat from Pearl Harbor was turned back 500 miles short of Howland due to bad weather and a few days later the Navy took charge of the search. During this time we ran down various false radio clues given by amateur radio operators. While the COLORADO searched the Phoenix group we searched to the West of this group and later on while the LEXINGTON searched to the North and West of Howland we searched the Gilbert group. In the meantime the SWAN searched various areas. In every case all intercepted messages by radio amateurs proved false as

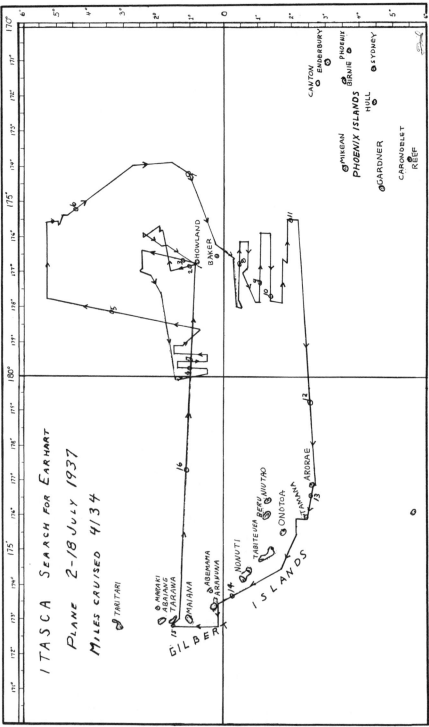

Fig. 6-5. The route the "Itasca" took in searching for Amelia. Official U.S. Coast Guard map. Courtesy National Archives.

did radio bearings on a carrier wave made by P.A.A. from Wake and Honolulu and at Howland Island.

Having exhausted all means and being out of fuel the search was abandoned on July 18, 1937, and after picking up the radio operator who was left on Howland we returned to Honolulu.

— END REPORT —

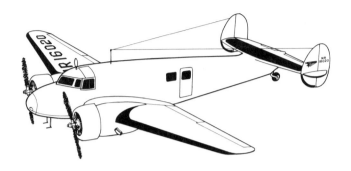

Chapter Seven
AMELIA PUSHED "THE-OUTSIDE-OF-THE-ENVELOPE"
She Was Determined To Succeed

"Outside-The-Envelope"

In retrospect, the events that occurred on Amelia's long over-water flight toward Howland Island expose several fatal errors in judgment. Amelia and navigator Fred Noonan, placed themselves and their aircraft "outside-the-(safety)-envelope."

"Outside-the-envelope" is an expression used when a device or vehicle is operating, beyond its normal performance, in a manner having the potential to cause an accident or disaster. For example, an automobile tire blowout immediately places the vehicle "outside-the-envelope" of its normal operation. The incident may or may not end in disaster. A device or vehicle performing within specifications is considered to be "inside-the-envelope."

The Inescapable Facts

We realize the following inescapable facts rob the world of the romantic myths that have persisted about Amelia Earhart over the last 58 years, but it is finally time to put them, and Amelia to rest. It is time to "set-the-record-straight."

1. We know that Amelia Earhart's *Electra* was *low on fuel* by her transmission to the *Itasca* at 7:41 AM, when she reported, "We must be on you but cannot see you but gas is running low. Been unable to reach you by radio. We are flying at 1,000 feet."

At 7:50 AM, she radioed, "We are circling but cannot hear you ...". Her transmissions at that time were very loud, at "S-5" level, indicating that she was very close to the ship; *probably within 50 miles.*

From the time of her low fuel report at 7:41 AM to her last transmission at 8:43 AM, Amelia obviously had a minimum of one hour and two minutes of fuel remaining. Circling the aircraft would have consumed even more fuel, bringing her no closer to the *Itasca.*

We do not know how much more fuel she had after 8:43 AM, if any, but the *Itasca* log shows clearly that she was excited and speaking very rapidly. It is safe to assume that she was becoming increasingly frightened and desperate.

Based on a takeoff at 10:00 AM (12:00 Noon Howland Island time) from Lae on the morning of July 1, and using her last radio transmission at 8:43 the following morning to the USCG *Itasca* waiting off Howland Island, Amelia and her navigator would have been in the air a total of 20 hours and 43 minutes; certainly longer than anticipated.

As the aircraft lightened with the burnoff of fuel and oil, airspeed would increase. However, strong headwinds, typical at that time of year, reduced groundspeed far below the projected rate of 150 MPH under favorable conditions. It is 2,556 miles from Lae to Howland Island. Assuming Amelia came within 50 miles of Howland before running out of fuel, she flew approximately 2,506 miles in 20 hours and 43 minutes at a rate of 122.66 MPH. Course corrections accounted for some of the lost time.

Also, leaning both engines to the maximum allowable would have added extra flight time. ("Leaning" means changing the fuel mixture to provide more air and less gasoline to the engines, conserving fuel.) Amelia knew how to handle both her engines to obtain minimum fuel consumption and most efficient performance. However, she had to be cautious when conserving her fuel. Leaning the engines excessively causes engine temperatures to rise, possibly resulting in engine failure.

Amelia was probably holding her fuel consumption rate down to approximately 50 gallons per hour. Considering the excess fuel consumed during the laborious takeoff from Lae, plus fuel used in her climb to cruising altitude, it is a virtual certainty she exhausted her 1,150 gallons of fuel short of her intended destination. She could have gained additional flying time and range by adding another 52 gallons to her tanks at Lae, bringing them up to absolute full capacity of 1,202 gallons, but the aircraft would have been too heavy for takeoff.

The portion of the military report referring to fuel consumption states (**National Archives Record Group 395**):

> Gasoline supply was estimated to last 24 hours with a possibility of lasting 30 hours. Judging from her last message at 0843 that she ran out of gas shortly thereafter as there were no more messages, her gasoline supply lasted approximately 21 hours — taking into account 1000 (Ed., 10:00 AM) takeoff at Lae and allowing 2 hours zone time difference between Lae and Howland. Judging that her estimated time of arrival at Howland was to be 0735 and the end of her gas supply at 0900 gives a gasoline safety factor of only 1 hour and 25 minutes, or approximately 7%.
>
> A gas reserve of 20% is usually required. Running the engines at a higher RPM than ordinary, or poor mixture control, would account for increased gasoline consumption.
>
> — END OF REPORT —

The military report estimated that Amelia's fuel lasted only 21 hours. Our estimate was just six minutes short of that figure at 20 hours, 54 minutes. Based on "actual flight time" from her Lae takeoff on 10:00 AM July 1, (12:00 Noon Howland Island time) her fuel supply actually lasted an additional one hour and 43 minutes. This estimate closely fits into the military air time frame estimated at between 24 and 30 hours.

As we previously calculated, the aircraft was only to stay airborne about 20 hours and 43 minutes. Amelia reported being low on fuel at 7:41 AM the next morning after leaving Lae. At that radio transmission time, 19 hours and 41 minutes would have elapsed since their takeoff from Lae.

Because Amelia's flight to Howland Island fell short of her estimated fuel range, we conclude that she was flying into strong headwinds, and she could have been having propeller pitch control difficulties.

2. We know that Amelia and Fred *did not have full use of their navigational equipment*. Noonan's chronometers were either inoperative or incorrectly set. Amelia's alternative was to navigate by dead reckoning. She was an excellent, highly competent dead reckoning navigator. Her midair course corrections and direction changes were amazingly accurate, since *Itasca* indicated, based on her incoming radio strengths, she was approaching quite close to the ship and Howland Island.

Since the *Electra* made no contact with the *Ontario* at the "point-of-no-return," Amelia was apparently too far off-course for her radio transmissions to reach the ship and, therefore she could not obtain a position fix from it. If the *Ontario* was transmitting on radio at 500 kilocycles, she could not hear its signals.

Most likely, many course corrections occurred all during the flight, consuming more precious fuel. The flight from Lae to Howland Island required more precise navigation than any other flight Amelia had ever undertaken. Although the leg from South America across the Atlantic to Africa was nearly as long, she had the entire length of a continent as a landing target.

Her arbitrary correction of Noonan's course, in that instance, cost them only a slight inconvenient delay. On her flight to Hawaii, the size and number of islands provided wide latitude for navigational error, and she had landmarks to guide her and the use of many radio frequencies on overland flights. There were no landmarks on the endless sea, and her target was no bigger, comparatively, than a pinhead.

3. We know that Amelia *could not use her 500 KC radio*. Thousands of miles before, she had either instructed its trailing antenna be cut off or had allowed it to be severed on

the advice of others. She and they did not realize that the 500 KC frequency was vital to her communications with ships.

Amelia either did not receive or ignored the telegram from the *Itasca* advising her to use the 500 KC frequency and also telling her which frequencies not to use. If she had sighted the *Ontario* but could not hear it on radio, she would have realized that she had serious radio problems. Her RDF (radio direction finder) was apparently not receiving properly, or she was not operating it correctly. Having ample fuel at "the-point-of-no-return," she could have returned safely to Lae for repair of her radio equipment.

If her RDF had been receiving properly, and had she retained the trailing antenna for her 500 KC radio, she could have homed in on *Itasca's* radio signals, since her transmission signals were coming to the ship "5 by 5," or loud and clear. This strong signal indicated she was flying toward the *Itasca* and Howland, probably within *50 or less miles.*

Had the *Itasca* been able to communicate with Amelia when her first transmission was received at 3:45 AM, she could have obtained weather and position information enabling her to fly directly to Howland Island. At 6:00 AM, she reported, "About 200 miles out." If she had left her transmitter "open," the ship could have figured a position fix on her, but she shut the transmitter off after each short report, saving her battery but preventing *Itasca's* radio operators from locating her, despite their heroic efforts.

It is possible that, had she not spent the next two hours blindly circling and searching for the *Itasca*, she may have had enough fuel and time to find and reach Howland Island. From the military report, we learned that the radio trans-mitter on Howland Island was not operating effectively, further complicating her perilous predicament.

Even if she had been able to hear the ship, Amelia's fuel may not have been sufficient to reach Howland Island. In that case, when she crashed into the sea the *Itasca* would have known her position and could have sped to her assistance. This, of course assumes she and Noonan were alive and the aircraft had stayed afloat for a few hours or, if the plane had sunk, they were able to use flotation devices. If the plane had sunk upon impact, which is probable, the outcome would have been the same. However, at least some chance of rescue existed if radio contact had been mutual.

Reassuring voices from the *Itasca* might have allayed Amelia's panic and helped her concentrate on reaching Howland. It would also have provided more time and support in preparing her to ditch the *Electra* in the water.

During her pre-flight training covering the *Electra* and its equipment, her technical advisor Paul Mantz had instructed Amelia on her radios and their specific uses, including that of the 500 KC radio to communicate with the *Ontario* and *Itasca*. Why she did not fully absorb or carry out his instructions will never be known. Perhaps her previous successes had made her overly confident, or she was distracted or inattentive during training sessions. *Unfortunately, lack of experience in use of her radio equipment, plus other unknown factors, proved to be her undoing.*

4. We know that during the entire flight from Lae to Howland Island *Amelia had no knowledge of upcoming weather conditions.* Since she had missed contact with the *Ontario*, she did not have the advantage of weather information relayed by the *Itasca*. Nearing the ship, she transmitted, "partly cloudy," and this condition would have made visual contact even more difficult. The *Itasca* transmitted weather and position information to Amelia almost constantly, but she could not hear it!

5. We know that *biological clock changes ("jet lag") affected the judgment of both Amelia Earhart and Fred Noonan.* It prevented them from performing at the optimum level necessary to overcome the obstacles to a successful flight from Lae to Howland Island.

The accumulated effects of physical, mental and emotional fatigue on the fliers during their Lae-Howland flight leg cannot be over-emphasized. After flying 21,000 miles without giving their bodies sufficient time and rest to adapt to time zone changes, they must have been "running-on-nerve" when they took off from Lae.

Some, if not all, of the errors in judgment committed by Amelia and Noonan during this flight leg are difficult to attribute to anything other than the stress and disorientation associated with "jet lag." This was no more true than when they failed to return to Lae after missing contact with the *Ontario* at the "point-of-no-return." *A pilot with Amelia's considerable experience would never have risked proceeding with the flight unless her judgment were impaired.*

Several times during the flight, Amelia and Fred must have lapsed into "micro-sleep," or naps, as the engines droned on, especially into the long night. During these lapses, the *Electra* would have drifted off course, requiring extensive navigational corrections and, again, consuming extra fuel.

The decision to fly from west-to-east, instead of east-to-west, as on her first world flight attempt, looms large in the tragedy of Amelia Earhart's loss. If the flight had occurred from Oakland to Hawaii to Howland to Lae, when Amelia and Fred were physically and mentally fresh, the remainder of the trip, with land legs or large landing targets, would have been relatively easy.

How Easy Is It To Ditch An Airplane?

In order to understand why it was so difficult for Amelia to safely ditch her aircraft in the open sea, we offer the following examples of actual ditching incidents to illustrate what can happen in an open sea ditching, with or without engine power. We will see that the probability of an aircraft flipping over under these conditions is extremely great.

Excerpts taken from the crash report of a Grumman G21A Air Boat, N-7777V, a twin-engine amphibian (sea plane), forced to ditch off the Island of St. Thomas in the US Virgin Islands on the morning of September 2, 1978, clearly show what can, and did, occur in this ditching accident. The pilot had a total of 42,005 flying hours to his credit, 5,233 of those flying the Grumman G21A Amphibian.

The following report is taken from records of the US National Transportation Safety Board, Washington, DC:

AIRCRAFT ACCIDENT REPORT - ANTILLES AIR BOATS, INC. GRUMMAN G21A, N-7777V, ST. THOMAS, VIRGIN ISLANDS, SEPTEMBER 2, 1978

FACTUAL INFORMATION

Flight 941 took off from St. Croix at 1003 A.S.T. (Atlantic Standard Time). The weather was VFR (Visual Flight Rules) with 25 miles visibility; the wind was 120 degrees at 12 knots. After takeoff, the aircraft flew at a cruising altitude of 1,700 feet MSL (above mean sea level). At 1017, when the aircraft was about 5 miles south of the St. Thomas seaplane ramp, the left engine failed. Passengers stated that they heard a loud "pop" or "clacking noise" which emanated from the left engine. The cowling was missing from the engine, and a dark object hung beneath the engine. Passengers who observed the captain stated that he immediately shut down the left engine and feathered the left propeller. They saw him advance the throttle of the right engine to maximum power setting. Although they did not feel the aircraft yaw to the left, at least one passenger stated that the aircraft was then flown with the left wing lower than the right wing.

The captain of N-48550, another Antilles Air Boat G21A, heard the exchange of transmissions between Flight 941 and the St. Thomas tower controller, and at 1020:34 transmitted, "Tower, this is Antilles 550. I've got him in sight. I'll stay with him." This captain stated that when he first saw Flight 941, it was about two miles south of Water Island, or about five miles from his position. He turned toward Flight 941, but as he approached, he saw it hit the water! At 1020:46, the captain of N-48550 transmitted, "Okay tower, let's get a rescue aircraft out immediately. He went in the water."

According to the captain of N-48550, Flight 941 landed to the northwest about six-tenths of a mile south of Water Island in the open sea. When the aircraft touched down it left a heavy spray of water behind it. After a "rollout" of 3 or 4 plane lengths, "a large explosive spray of water occurred, the aircraft appeared to cartwheel on its left wing, and momentarily disappeared from my view." Initially he saw no survivors but soon saw them appear around the wreckage. He circled the accident site and attempted to guide pleasure and fishing boats to the area. He stated, "The water was quite choppy with many whitecaps handicapping visual observation."

The passenger in the right cockpit seat recalled that the airspeed indicated about 100 MPH during the descent. He also observed a 300-400 FPM (feet per minute) rate of descent on the vertical speed indicator. The captain had his left hand on the control wheel, and his right hand on the right throttle until impact. As the aircraft approached the water, the airspeed was still about 100 MPH. The passenger in the right cockpit seat saw whitecaps on the water and high sea swells. He believed that the right engine was being operated at a high power setting as the aircraft hit the water. Another passenger recalled 5 to 6 ft. swells, which were moving from the southeast.

Other passengers also believed that the aircraft was approaching the water at a fast speed. Some passengers recalled that the aircraft was level at impact; some recalled that the right wing was down. The impact was hard and the aircraft bounced. Most passengers stated that after the first bounce, the captain placed both hands on the control wheel and turned it to the left. When the aircraft struck the water, the left wing dug into the water and the aircraft cartwheeled, pivoting on the left wing.

The aircraft broke apart after the cartwheel and sank within a few minutes. The aircraft came to rest on the bottom of the ocean in 85 feet of water.

— END OF REPORT —

Fig. 7-1. This Grumman G21A twin-engine amphibian, powered by two Pratt and Whitney Wasp Jr. R985 model engines (similar to those installed on Amelia Earhart's Lockheed Electra), is the same model that crashed in the Virgin Islands on September 2, 1978. Gomez photo.

This accident occurred in daylight hours and with heavy whitecap sea swells. The captain and three of the ten passengers died in this crash. The aircraft was destroyed and sank within minutes.

In contrast to the Grumman Antilles Air Boat crash off the Virgin Islands in 1978, an example of a more successful mid-ocean ditching is that of Pan American Flight 943 in October of 1956.

The captain of this Boeing B-377 Stratocruiser was on a non-stop flight from Honolulu, Hawaii to California with 26 passengers and crew aboard. At approximately mid-flight, he experienced a failure of two of his four engines, preventing completion of the flight.

On station nearby the midway point in this flight was the U.S. Coast Guard cutter *Ponchartrain.* The communication between the Coast Guard ship and Flight 943 was excellent. Ditching intentions were established and nothing was left to chance.

The Pan American captain had never ditched at sea, but he had been properly trained on what procedures to follow and had reviewed many "open sea" ditching training films. He was also fortunate to be flying a land plane which, by reason of design, made the ocean ditching better than most land planes. Even so, the entire tail section of the Boeing broke off before the aircraft had completed a full stop on the water.

Actual movies taken during the ditching operation indicate that a proper water landing is possible in a land plane, provided the sea is calm and the actual ditching is performed correctly. Recommended procedure for ditching in heavy seas is to set down parallel to the swells even if it is a crosswind landing.

In this particular incident, the sea was very calm and just to be certain it would remain that way, the Coast Guard ship laid down a blanket of foam on the water. Flight 943 made a "picture-book-perfect" ditch, yet the tail section broke off upon impact and the aircraft sank within minutes. The captain ditched his aircraft very close to the Coast Guard ship and their rapid deployment of rescue personnel and lifeboats was instrumental in the successful rescue of all the passengers and crew of Flight 943. If it had not been for the Coast Guard ship contact, this open Pacific Ocean ditching may have ended in tragedy.

Amelia's Final Anguished Hours

When Amelia Earhart ditched her Lockheed *Electra* in open ocean sea swells, she had no experience or training in ditching either a land or seaplane. There was no room for error. She had neither the comfort of a nearby ship or an aircraft overhead to report her condition and position. She was on her own, seeing nothing but squally weather and rough seas, as reported by the captain of the *Itasca*.

Using official records and all other available information, we will attempt to re-create the events of Amelia Earhart's final anguished hours.

Radio silence was broken 15 hours and 45 minutes into the flight. Sometime prior to Amelia's first radio message to the *Itasca* at 3:45 AM, (on 3105 KC, a radio frequency *Itasca* had asked her not to use) she may have been napping. Upon awakening, she made course corrections, using dead reckoning navigation, based on her estimate of the *Electra's* position at that time. Believing, correctly, that she was nearing the *Itasca* and Howland Island, she passed a message to Fred Noonan asking him to help her locate their destination; or he may have passed a message to her offering to help. Noonan would have crawled forward from his rear navigator's station, over the top of the fuselage fuel tanks, to take a position in the right-hand co-pilot's seat.

When they had almost reached the *Itasca*, Amelia reported she was at 1,000 feet, circling, but she could not hear the ship's radio. She continued to search for the ship or Howland until the *Electra, a land plane*, ran out of fuel and started down toward the ocean. The *Itasca* never received a "mayday" distress signal from either Earhart or Noonan.

When Lockheed NR-16020 descended with Amelia at the controls, she had very little choice or control over how and where the aircraft contacted the water. Heavy seas would have caused her height above the water to vary considerably, and it would have proven very difficult to judge if smooth conditions had prevailed. Water surfaces play tricks with judgment of height above the water. Out of fuel, with no engine power, she could only flat glide until setting down on the water.

On hitting the unpredictable sea, the *Electra* either cart-wheeled or flipped over on its back. The sudden stop tore the internal auxiliary fuel tanks loose from their hold-down straps, slamming them forward and pinning Amelia in the front cockpit. If Noonan had moved forward, he would have been similarly trapped.

If they had escaped the onslaught of the loose fuel tanks, they would have faced grave difficulties in trying to escape through the top hatch of the *Electra*. Figure 7-2 of Amelia standing in the open hatch above the cockpit shows how narrow it is. It opened up and over to the right, so only one person at a time could have crawled out. The hatch opens directly behind the loop antenna. There is no second hatch over the right front cockpit seat. The same open hatch can be seen in the crash photos taken at Luke Field when Amelia groundlooped the *Electra* during her first world flight attempt.

Fig. 7-2. Amelia Earhart standing in the open forward hatch of her Lockheed *Electra*; dark strip just behind Amelia is actually the top portion of the open hatch. National Archives photo.

With the aircraft inverted in the sea, it would have been virtually impossible for her and Noonan to exit the *Electra* through the narrow opening in the single hatch.

Water pressure on the outside of the hatch would have prevented its opening from the inside unless Amelia had opened it before contact with the water, in which case onrushing sea water would have prevented escape. While totally occupied with trying to control the aircraft, it is doubtful she would have thought of opening the hatch.

The fuselage fuel tanks could have torn from their mounts and ruptured and they, along with the cabin, would have quickly filled with water. Amelia's 20 hour and 43 minute flight had consumed all the fuel aboard. Prop pitch changes and engine oil leaks enroute, a typical experience during previous legs of the journey, had certainly reduced the remaining oil supply. *This would indicate there was little or no fuel or oil to leave much of a slick for searchers to see.*

Had Amelia's aircraft broken-up upon ditching, some trace of it or its contents would probably have remained afloat. However, nothing was found on the surface or on any of the islands in the vicinity.

The only possible explanation is that the *Electra*, along with Amelia Earhart and Fred Noonan, quickly sank in 19,000 feet of water, somewhere in the vicinity of Howland Island.

Itasca personnel waited until 10:00 the morning of July 2, 1937 and then became part of the most extensive naval search in history. Realizing Amelia had run out of fuel, the *Itasca* began an immediate search totaling 4,134 miles. It covered quadrants in the north, south, east and west of Howland Island.

The US Navy battleship *Colorado* searched the Phoenix Island Group located southeast of Howland and found nothing. The *Itasca* search pattern, which also included all of the Gilbert Island Group, turned-up nothing. Search aircraft from the carrier *Lexington* covered a wide search area and reported no contact with either the downed *Electra* or her crew. Every available ship was dispatched to the area to assist in the search, to no avail.

Our purpose is not to denigrate the monumental accomplishments of Amelia Earhart or criticize her actions on her second world flight attempt. Our intent is to analyze the facts in order to establish rational conclusions regarding her fate.

We must remember that Amelia had much less experience in flying the twin-engine *Electra,* a more complex aircraft, than she had in her previous single-engine *Vega.* Much of her *Electra's* on-board equipment was experimental (she called it her "flying laboratory"). The state of radio, weather and navigation technology in 1937 was primitive compared to today's sophisticated equipment. Also, we now know about the detrimental effects of "biological clock" changes on the human body and mind.

A combination of adverse factors and circumstances caused Amelia Earhart's death. Her determination, strength and courage were not enough to save her. The odds were just too great for her to succeed in her attempt to be the first woman to fly around the world.

From all evidence from every reliable source, from July 1, 1937 until now, only one possible solution can be found to the "mystery" of Amelia Earhart's disappearance. After running out of fuel, Amelia, Fred Noonan and their Lockheed Electra NR-16020, plunged into the Pacific and vanished almost immediately into its depths only a few miles from the Itasca and Howland Island.

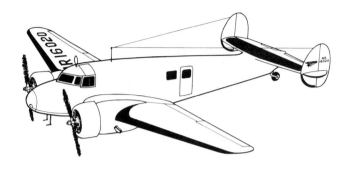

Chapter Eight
THE IMPLAUSIBLE JAPANESE CONNECTION
And Other Fables And Myths

During our years of research for this book, we encountered many conflicting theories about Amelia Earhart's disappearance during her second world flight attempt. These theories have added to the mystique, but none has proven to be credible. Some of the originators of these theories spent years researching locales and materials, sometimes at great financial cost, to support their pet notions. All led to dead ends!

The Implausible Japanese Connection

The most widely publicized theory regarding the disappearance of Amelia Earhart is that she and Fred Noonan somehow reached the Japanese-held island of Saipan, 2,500 miles northwest of Howland Island. After crash landing on Saipan, the story goes, they were taken prisoner and executed prior to the invasion of Saipan by US Marines in 1944.

Another version of this gigantic "geographical leap" of 2,500 miles from the vicinity of Howland Island to Saipan is that Amelia and her navigator seriously erred in their navigation to the extent they were actually 175 miles northeast of Howland when they reported being low on fuel. While searching hopelessly for Howland, they crashed on Mili

Atoll of Barre Island in the Japanese occupied Marshall Islands. They were then taken back to Saipan and imprisoned. In this scenario, Amelia died of dysentery and Noonan was executed.

Some former marines stated they found Amelia's briefcase containing her log book and flight charts in a Japanese safe on Saipan. These items, they claim, were turned over to a high-ranking military officer and never seen again. They also stated that they found her Lockheed *Electra* in a nearby hangar but, soon after being discovered, it was consumed by a mysterious fire.

According to reports from Saipan natives, an American man and woman were executed by the Japanese military before the U.S. invasion. Although their grave sites were supposedly located years later, no bones were found upon excavation. A remnant of cloth said to be the blindfold worn by the woman before being shot was the only "evidence" produced by her purported grave.

While it is, of course, remotely possible that an undetermined number of American men and women were captured and killed by the Japanese on Saipan at some time, Amelia Earhart and Fred Noonan were assuredly not among them.

On October 16, 1937, an Australian newspaper, *Smiths Weekly*, ran a front page story indicating that the search for Amelia Earhart by U.S. Navy ships and aircraft gave them the opportunity to sweep close enough to Japanese-mandated islands. The article claimed this enabled the ships and planes to observe Japanese naval activities. At a League of Nations peace conference after World War I, Pacific islands were mandated (put under the control of) several countries. Islands mandated to Japan were the Mariannes, Marshalls, Carolines and Yap.

On January 17, 1938, U.S. Senator Gerald P. Nye sent a copy of the *Smith's Weekly* article to then Secretary of State Cordell Hull, who responded on January 20, 1938 that the U.S. naval and air search was far removed from Japanese-mandated islands.

Copies of the Nye-Hull correspondence follow (National Archives and Record Service).

SPECIAL MESSENGER

FL

GLASS, VA., CHAIRMAN
KELLAR, TENN.
S. COPELAND, N. Y.
CARL DEN, ARIZ.
ELMER THOMAS, OKLA.
JAMES F. BYRNES, S. C.
MILLARD E. TYDINGS, MD.
RICHARD B. RUSSELL, JR., GA.
ALVA B. ADAMS, COLO.
PATRICK MC CARRAN, NEV.
JOHN H. OVERTON, LA.
JOHN H. BANKHEAD, ALA.
JOSEPH C. O'MAHONEY, WYO.
WILLIAM GIBBS MC ADOO, CALIF.
HARRY S. TRUMAN, MO.
F. RYAN DUFFY, WIS.
EDWARD R. BURKE, NEBR.
HERBERT E. HITCHCOCK, S. DAK.
THEODORE F. GREEN, R. I.

FREDERICK HALE, MAINE
GERALD P. NYE, N. DAK.
FREDERICK STEIWER, OREG.
JOHN G. TOWNSEND, JR., DEL.
H. STYLES BRIDGES, N. H.

KENNEDY F. REA, CLERK
JOHN W. R. SMITH, ASST. CLERK

United States Senate

COMMITTEE ON APPROPRIATIONS

RECEIVED DEPARTMENT OF STATE 1938 JAN 1 PM 3 31

DIVISION OF COMMUNICATIONS AND RECORDS

January 17, 1938

Answered HCR

Division of FAR EASTERN AFFAIRS JAN 1 1938 Department of State

JAN 19 1938 DEPARTMENT OF STATE

862i.01 note 800.79611 Putnam, Amelia Earhart

* Honorable Cordell Hull
Department of State
Washington, D. C.

8621.01/333

Dear Mr. Secretary:

I am sending you, herewith, photograph of the front page of "Smith's Weekly", published in Sydney, Australia. The continuation of the article starting on that page is completed on a second photostat which accompanies the first. I know you will find interest in reading this article if you have not already done so.

I am submitting it to you, first, for the information which it may afford; and second, to ascertain whatever might be available concerning the authenticity of the article. I am especially anxious to know if the story has any foundation in fact at all; whether the findings, if any, made by the Navy Fliers were substantial; and whether it is true that the alleged findings were shared with the British Navy?

You need not bother to return the photostats referred to since I am holding an additional one for my own use and information.

FILED JAN 21 1938

Sincerely yours,

Gerald P. Nye

Encl

F/A

* National Archives and Record Service.

Fig. 8-1. Senator Gerald Nye's letter to Secretary of State Cordell Hull regarding the *Smith's Weekly* newspaper article.

Fig. 8-2. The *Smith's Weekly* newspaper article which Secretary Hull refuted in his letter to Senator Nye.

January 20 1938

In reply refer to
FE 8621.01/333

* My dear Senator Nye:

    I am in receipt of your letter of January 17,
1938, enclosing a photostatic copy of an article
headed "U.S.A. does AUSTRALIA a Secret Service", from
the October 16, 1937 issue of Smith's Weekly, published in Sydney, Australia. This article deals
chiefly with the search made by the United States Navy
air force for Miss Amelia Earhart, whose plane was
thought to have been forced down somewhere between
Gilbert Islands and Howland Island in the North Pacific,
and the alleged seizure by the United States Navy of
this opportunity to survey the Japanese mandated islands in that area.

                                                    Its

The Honorable

        Gerald P. Nye,

            United States Senate.

8621.01/333

F/FG

* National Archives and Record Service.

Fig. 8-3. Secretary of State Hull's letter to Senator Nye refuting that the search for Amelia
was a cover-up to survey Japanese mandated islands.

-2-

It is the understanding of the Department that
the allegations in the article concerning which you
inquire are without foundation since the area covered
in the search for Miss Earhart was considerably removed
from that occupied by the Japanese mandated islands.

The courtesy which prompted you to make the article
available to the Department is appreciated.

Sincerely yours,

Cordell Hull

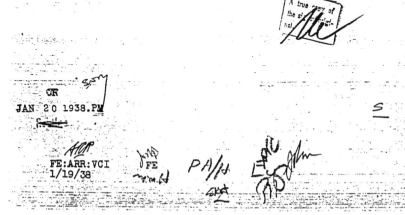

FE:ARR:VCI
1/19/38

Fig. 8-4. Page two of Hull's letter to Nye.

Secretary Hull refutes the *Smith's Weekly* contention that the search for Amelia Earhart was, in fact, an American excuse to overfly and observe Japanese naval activities in and around island groups under their control prior to World War II.

The Japanese were undoubtedly acutely aware that the world flight of Amelia Earhart and Fred Noonan would pass in close proximity to their mandated Pacific islands. *As soon as the two fliers were reported down and missing, the Japanese government co-operated in the search within their territorial waters, and they reported finding no trace of the missing aircraft or crew. Should they have found Amelia and Fred, they would certainly have turned them over to American authorities, avoiding the possibility of U.S. ships or aircraft searching close to the Japanese islands. In all of the reported air and sea searches, there is no mention of any contact with Japanese aircraft or surface vessels.*

If the United States government had discovered that the Japanese had captured Amelia Earhart and Fred Noonan, a serious break in diplomacy could have resulted between the two countries at a time of extremely delicate relations. The spotlight of world publicity would surely have shone on the secret Japanese military build-up in the Pacific in preparation for their attack on Pearl Harbor in 1941.

Another slant on the "Saipan Theory" is that Amelia's world flight was merely a smokescreen masking her assignment from the U.S. government to spy on Japanese Pacific military installations. This, simply is not true! *First, Amelia's Lockheed carried no "spy equipment," and, second, the Lockheed bore full outside identification, strange indeed for a "spy plane." No evidence of any kind has ever been found to indicate that Amelia was involved in undercover government activities.*

Amelia Earhart was a revered figure in every corner of the world. If the Japanese had captured and killed her, exposure of their actions would have united an outraged world against them, causing an incident of gigantic proportions at a time when the Japanese wished to appear co-operative and peaceloving. It is totally irrational to believe they would have become involved in harming a famous U.S. aviatrix at a time when they were trying to maintain utmost secrecy in their Pacific military operations.

The California Crash

In 1970, a book was authored by Joe Klaas and Joseph Gervais entitled *Amelia Earhart Lives* claiming that Amelia Earhart's Lockheed *Electra* had recently crashed on a California mountainside. As proof of this claim, three photographs were shown of a crashed aircraft. The top and middle photos are captioned, "Official F.A.A. photos taken on the California mountainside which clearly show the registration N-16020, the same as that of the Lockheed *Electra* of Amelia's last flight." The bottom photo is captioned, "The exhaust manifold plate found in the above wreckage. Note the delivery date May 5, 1937."

Upon close examination of these photos, the identification number of the downed aircraft is shown partially. The remainder of the number is obscured.

The authors stated that the aircraft bore the number N-16020. Amelia Earhart's *Electra* bore I.D. number NR-16020. "N" is not "NR," the important difference being the "R," which stands for "restricted." In this case, "restricted" indicates that this number was reserved exclusively and permanently for Amelia Earhart and was never issued to anyone other than Amelia Earhart.

In 1989, we wrote to the Federal Aviation Administration requesting registration and ownership information on combinations of the number "16020" with several letter prefixes. We then wrote the FAA for registration information on similar numbers "16320," "16820" and "16920." We selected these numbers because the third from last number in one of the aforementioned photos is partly visible and by its top curve could be one of these numbers.

Our letters to the FAA and the FAA replies follow.

P.O. Box 3431
Sebring, Florida
33871
March 3, 1989

Mr. Mike Monroney
Federal Aviation Administration
Aeronautical Center
Aircraft Registration Branch, AVN - 450
P.O. Box 25082
Oklahoma City, Oklahoma 73125

Dear Mr. Monroney,

I am researching some old Lockheed Aircraft of the 1937 period. I ran across several aircraft registration numbers which I would like to correctly know who the aircraft was registered to.

Again I say, the year was on or about 1937 and the aircraft were Lockheed Electra models 10A and 10E. Following are the three numbers I am interested in:

N-16020 ... NR-16020
and
R-16020

Any information on the type aircraft, model number and owners at time of their registration, would be greatly appreciated. I am enclosing a self addressed stamped envelope for your convenience.

Sincerely,

Walter E. Roessler

Walter E. Roessler

Fig. 8-5. Co-author Roessler's letter to the FAA is researching aircraft registration numbers that might have been mistaken as the one on Amelia's *Electra*. Note: The Mike Monroney Aeronautical Center of the FAA was named in honor of the Oklahoma Congressman. (He did not work at the facility, which the authors were unaware of.)

P.O. Box 3431
Sebring, Florida
33871
April 18, 1989

Mr. Mike Monroney
Federal Aviation Administration
Aeronautical Center
Aircraft Registration Branch, AVN-450
P.O. Box 25082
Oklahoma City, Oklahoma 73125

Dear Mr. Monroney,

Thank you for your reply letter dated 4/11/89 concerning aircraft ownership of NR16020.

I am now in need of the following information if your Department is able to furnish same. I would like to correctly know, who the following aircraft were registered to and the last or latest date of registration:

N-16320   N-16820

and

N-16920

I am, as I mentioned in my first letter, doing some research on old Lockheed aircraft, although, the above registration numbers will certainly be of great help.

I am enclosing a self addressed stamped envelope for your reply and convenience.

Sincerely,

Walter E. Roessler

Fig. 8-6. Another letter from co-author Roessler to the FAA regarding aircraft registration numbers similar to the one on Amelia's *Electra*.

DEPARTMENT OF TRANSPORTATION
FEDERAL AVIATION ADMINISTRATION

DATE: April 11, 1989

IN REPLY
REFER TO: AAC-250

MIKE MONRONEY AERONAUTICAL CENTER
P.O. BOX 25082
OKLAHOMA CITY, OKLAHOMA 73125

SUBJECT: Your request of March 3, 1989

FROM: FAA Aircraft Registry

TO: Walter E. Roessler
P.O. Box 3431
Sebring, Florida 33871

/ /   Complete information concerning registration of aircraft is contained
in Part 47 of the Federal Aviation Regulations. Lien recordation
information is in Part 49. Copies may be ordered from the Superintendent
of Documents, U.S. Government Printing Office, Washington, D.C. 20402.

/ /   We prefer that you use the security instrument which is approved locally;
however, if the enclosed AC Form 8050-98, Aircraft Security Agreement,
meets the pertinent provisions of your local statutes, it may be used.
This form may be reproduced.

/ /   If you will furnish a description of the aircraft for which you have
not received the recording acknowledgment, we will complete and send
AC Form 8050-41, Part I-Conveyance Recordation Notice, Part II-Release,
for these aircraft.

/ /   We are unable to identify the aircraft from the description given. Please
furnish make, model, serial number, and registration number. Return the
enclosed correspondence with your reply.

/ /   A supply of the forms you requested is maintained in your FAA District
Office (see enclosed list).

/ /   We have authorized the Regional Disbursing Office to refund your
remittance. Please allow 4 to 6 weeks for receipt.

/XX/   Lockheed Electra model 10E, NR16020 was used by Amelia Earhart. As you
probably know, the number 16020 has been reserved for her on a permanent
basis. Our records show no other registrations of that number for a
Lockheed Electra.

Sincerely,

Roy E. Franklin
Aircraft Registration Clerk
Enclosure

AC 8050-69 (12-80) (0052-00-588-5000) Supersedes previous edition

Fig. 8-7. A letter to co-author Roessler clearly indicating that the aircraft registration with the numbers 16020 were reserved for Amelia's *Electra* on a permanent basis.

```
DATE -  04/28/89   --- AIRCRAFT INQUIRY SCREEN ---     TIME -  13:59
AIRCRAFT DESCRIPTION                         CHG-NUMBER - DATE
=======================                      ====================
REG-NUMBER: 16320 ✓                          PENDING NR CHG TO :
SER NUMBER: 28-7305225                       DATE AUTHORIZED   :
YEAR-MAKE :  73 PIPER                         TYPE REGISTRATION : INDVL
MODEL     : PA-28-180                         CERT ISSUE DATE   : 01-03-85
REGISTERED OWNER:                            LAST ACTIVITY DATE: 02-24-87
==================
NAME      : HANOVER FLYERS INC               ACTUAL  CERT  DATE: --
STREET    : PO BOX 1286                      DEALER            : NO
CITY      : MATTITUCK                        ARRAS ACCESS CODE : 240420
STATE-ZIP : NY    11952                      ARRAS/CONV        : C
COUNTRY   : US                               BATCH-ID          :
STATUS    : * - VALID                        BATCH-STATUS      :
OTHER OWNERS: NONE                           SUSP-FLAG         :
01                             06
02                             07
03                             08
04                             09
05                             10
AIRWORTHINESS DATE:          CLASS: STANDARD            CAT:
ENGINE MAKE: LYCOMING        ENGINE MODEL: O&VO-360 SER


HARDCOPY USER ARACH     ON H01LEA7  (00246) MVS/XA    13:59:41 04/28/89
DATE -  04/28/89   --- AIRCRAFT INQUIRY SCREEN ---     TIME -  13:59
AIRCRAFT DESCRIPTION                         CHG-NUMBER - DATE
=======================                      ====================
REG-NUMBER: 16820 ✓                          PENDING NR CHG TO :
SER NUMBER: 2830                             DATE AUTHORIZED   :
YEAR-MAKE :  36 FAIRCHILD                     TYPE REGISTRATION : COOWN
MODEL     : 24 C8E                           CERT ISSUE DATE   : 05-11-76
REGISTERED OWNER:                            LAST ACTIVITY DATE: 07-27-88
==================
NAME      : NELSON ROBERT S                  ACTUAL  CERT  DATE: 07-27-88
STREET    : PO BOX 140                       DEALER            : NO
CITY      : EASTSOUND                        ARRAS ACCESS CODE : 292220
STATE-ZIP : WA    98245                      ARRAS/CONV        : C
COUNTRY   : US                               BATCH-ID          :
STATUS    : * - VALID                        BATCH-STATUS      :
OTHER OWNERS: 1                              SUSP-FLAG         :
01 NELSON CRAIG M              06
02                             07
03                             08
04                             09
05                             10
AIRWORTHINESS DATE: 07-03-58  CLASS: STANDARD           CAT:
ENGINE MAKE: WARNER          ENGINE MODEL: SS40&50


HARDCOPY USER ARACH     ON H01LEA7  (00246) MVS/XA    14:00:07 04/28/89
DATE -  04/28/89   --- AIRCRAFT INQUIRY SCREEN ---     TIME -  14:00
AIRCRAFT DESCRIPTION                         CHG-NUMBER - DATE
=======================                      ====================
REG-NUMBER: 16920 ✓                          PENDING NR CHG TO :
SER NUMBER: 30865                            DATE AUTHORIZED   :
YEAR-MAKE :  77 BELL                          TYPE REGISTRATION : CORP
MODEL     : 212                              CERT ISSUE DATE   : 09-04-85
REGISTERED OWNER:                            LAST ACTIVITY DATE: 08-20-88
==================
NAME      : TEMSCO HELICOPTERS INC           ACTUAL  CERT  DATE: --
STREET    : PO BOX 5057                      DEALER            : NO
CITY      : KETCHIKAN                        ARRAS ACCESS CODE : 732240
STATE-ZIP : AK    99901                      ARRAS/CONV        : C
COUNTRY   : US                               BATCH-ID          :
STATUS    : A - VALID                        BATCH-STATUS      :
OTHER OWNERS: NONE                           SUSP-FLAG         :
01                             06
02                             07
03                             08
04                             09
05                             10
AIRWORTHINESS DATE: 12-05-77  CLASS: STANDARD           CAT: T
ENGINE MAKE: U/A CANADA      ENGINE MODEL: PT6 SER 578HP
```

Fig. 8-8. Aircraft Inquiry Screen showing who owned the aircraft with registration numbers 16320, 16820 and 16920.

Nonetheless, Klaas and Gervais expect us to believe that Amelia's Lockheed somehow found its way back to the United States after her disappearance. Obviously, they did not bother to verify their information in writing their book.

The Gardner Island (Nikumaroro) Fantasy

In January of 1992, an organization named TIGHAR (The International Group for Historic Aircraft Recovery), led by Richard Gillespie, reported that in October, 1991, they had found conclusive proof that Amelia Earhart and Fred Noonan landed on an outer, low-lying coral reef off Gardner Island (now known as Nikumaroro) in the Phoenix Island Group, 425 miles southeast of Howland Island. Gillespie stated they were in the process of conclusively identifying their "find." They said they were "90% sure" that the items they had found on the island belonged to Amelia Earhart or her aircraft.

This group postulates that Amelia somehow located Nikumaroro Island and landed her plane on the reef, where it remained for three days before wave action, or a sudden storm, washed it into the ocean. They further claim that she transmitted distress signals during that three day period. They assume that Amelia and Fred, suffering sweltering temperatures, died on the island from lack of food and water.

This is the same group that found a metal box on Nikumaroro Island in 1989, claiming that it was Fred Noonan's navigation chart case, or one similar to that carried on Amelia Earhart's *Electra*. After much media hoopla over this event, nothing more was heard of it, and the box was never identified as coming from Amelia's aircraft.

In March of 1992, TIGHAR again received national media coverage to at last reveal their latest "find," consisting of: 1) part of a size "9" shoe, 2) a screw-type medicine bottle cap of purported U.S. manufacture, and 3) a piece of metal, bearing a rivet pattern, which they said washed up on the shore of Nikumaroro Island and became lodged in the sand, where they found it.

Of course, they claim that the piece of metal is part of the outer "skin" of Amelia Earhart's Lockheed *Electra*. They say it's a patch placed on the *Electra's* underbelly at the Lockheed factory, after she groundlooped it in Hawaii during her first world flight attempt. In addition, they boasted that they are "going-back-after-the-airplane" in the near future.

It is difficult to understand how such an obvious hoax can be countenanced as legitimate by our national print and television media.

In refutation of the TIGHAR claims, we offer the following:

For the moment, we will set aside the "hard evidence" found by the expedition and consider the most important question. Was it possible for Amelia Earhart to reach Nikumaroro Island? The answer is an emphatic "No!".

Amelia Earhart's last transmissions, her own words, answer the question. She said she was "running-low-on-fuel." She said she was "circling." Her transmissions, faithfully reproduced from the log of the U.S. Coast Guard cutter *Itasca* earlier in our book, are our only clues. Her transmissions were coming to the *Itasca* "S-5" or "5 by 5," (loud and clear), indicating by their strength and clarity that she was very close to the ship. Obviously, however, she did not know her position.

In an article in the April, 1992 issue of *Life* magazine, Richard Gillespie states that Amelia "asked for a signal on a very high frequency. The *Itasca* sent the signal. *She received it* (authors' italics), but her radio was unable to home in on high frequency transmissions..." Amelia's 500 KC radio was inoperative! If Amelia had received any voice messages from the *Itasca*, or even one usable signal, she would have known she was near Howland Island. Knowing that she would have continued looking for Howland rather than flying off to a far-distant Nikumaroro. *Furthermore, it would be inconceivable that she would make the decision to leave the Howland area without notifying the Itasca she intended to fly to Nikumaroro and without requesting they start rescue efforts.*

Next, there is the matter of distance. On the Pacific Ocean map shown in the *Life* article, the distance between Howland Island and Nikumaroro appears to be a short hop. Not so; it is *425 miles away!* We know the fuel load on the *Electra* and we know its approximate groundspeed to be 122 MPH from its flying time from Lae to Howland Island. Amelia would be trying to conserve fuel, so her groundspeed would be even slower in attempting to reach Nikumaroro, particularly at 1,000 feet, her last reported altitude.

Even at 122 MPH, it would have taken her 3 hours and 50 minutes to reach Nikumaroro. At a normal cruising speed of 150 MPH, the trip would take 2 hours and 50 minutes. At the *Electra's* full-throttle, high fuel consumption speed of 165 MPH, it would have required 2 hours, 35 minutes.

Gillespie says that "Noonan could be sure that, even if he missed Howland, he would reach the island in the Phoenix group in about two hours." In that two hours, the *Electra* would have to fly that 425 miles at 212.5 MPH, ie., with a hefty 62 MPH tailwind, provided, of course, two hours of fuel remained.

In our combined 67 years of aviation experience, we have never known a pilot to report "low-on-fuel" with more than 30 minutes of fuel remaining. Allowing the 30 minutes to Amelia Earhart, she could not have gone more than another 83 miles if she had pushed the *Electra* to 165 MPH, consuming fuel in huge quantities. She was also consuming more fuel as she circled, just trying to determine her position.

Was Amelia Earhart lying when she reported "low on fuel?" To question the veracity of a pilot under these extreme emergency conditions is absurd. The Itasca reported that Amelia sounded increasingly agitated and desperate. Contemplating flying another 425 miles to Nikumaroro would unquestionably make her even more so.

As to Amelia's last report, "We are on the line 157/337 ... We are running on line," there is no way to tell whether Noonan's instruments were accurate. Gillespie says, "I traced the line on the chart and read the name of the island: Nikumaroro."

At this point, Amelia would have had five factors to consider.

1. Sextant error (time of day).
2. Directional gyro drift.
3. Variation of the magnetic North Pole.
4. Compass deviation.
5. Wind drift conditions.

If any of the preceeding factors were calculated incorrectly, particularly considering Amelia's and Fred's fatigue and biological clock change (jet lag) status, the information transmitted to the *Itasca* regarding her track line (157/337) would have been grossly erroneous.

The *Itasca's* weather reports showed cloudy, squally weather to the northwest. If Amelia was lost, did not know her position and could not find Howland, how could she have found Nikumaroro? These questions, and the facts, cannot be ignored.

Amelia simply did not have enough fuel to reach Niku-maroro. Any other so-called "evidence" unearthed by Gillespie's expedition is rendered meaningless by that one irrefutable fact.

However, we may as well explore Gillespie's other claims. Now we come to Amelia's landing on the coral reef near the island. No pilot would for an instant consider landing, wheels down, on a coral reef! Despite Gillespie's description of the reef as a "level table of hard coral," the surface of coral is sharp and jagged, having many crevices or gaps. It can tear an airplane apart.

Amelia had no experience with emergency sea or island landings, but Noonan had flown all over the Pacific and would have known what all island-hopping pilots know. A belly-ripping reef is the last place a pilot would land. The landing site of choice is on a beach parallel to the shore or on a beach heading straight inland.

Richard Gillespie had to conjure up the reef landing to make the *Electra* disappear by falling off, or being swept off, the reef into the ocean after three days, before a search of the area. Otherwise, the entire airplane, or pieces of it, would still be sitting on the beach or the island itself (or on exhibit at the Smithsonian). It would have been easily seen during the most casual air search.

If Amelia had found a reef smooth as glass and managed to land her airplane intact, could she have sent distress signals for three days, as Gillespie says? The military investigative report on Amelia Earhart's flight from Lae to Howland Island (**National Archives, Record Group 395**) states that Pan

American Airways in Hawaii transmitted a message to Amelia Earhart via radio and asked her to respond with four dashes if she heard them. They claimed to have heard four dashes which they pinpointed as coming from Gardner. (Nikumaroro). *Not only did Amelia not use or carry Morse Code radio equipment on her aircraft, but her batteries, if at all usable, would never have been strong enough to relay any type of response back to Hawaii over 1,000 miles away.*

"Earhart's signal, barely audible but persistent," says Gillespie, "was picked up by HMS *Achilles* and by stations all over the Pacific." *While hundreds of reports were heard from all over the Pacific, including many from ham radio operators, that they had received signals from Amelia Earhart, U.S. government agencies traced each and every one of them, and none proved to be valid.*

Also, because of the high volume of radio transmissions in the area at the time, frequencies were so heavily-used that transmissions by Amelia, if she made any, would have been lost in the traffic. *The military report shows that these bogus reports interfered with their attempts to reach Amelia.*

As to Gillespie's reference to a report from the U.S. battleship *Colorado* that one of their personnel saw "signs of recent habitation," it is possible that not every single soul whoever set foot on Nikumaroro reported their presence to the world.

Back to the size "9" shoe, bottle cap and piece of metal. When an Earhart biographer, Doris Rich, during a television interview with Richard Gillespie, said that Amelia Earhart wore a size "7" shoe, not a size "9," Gillespie replied that "people's shoe sizes can change;" a lame retort indeed.

As for the bottle cap, it would not be unusual for a U.S. medicine bottle to belong to one of the British who put a work party on the island a year after Amelia supposedly landed there. The bottle could have been washed ashore and swept inland by one of Gillespie's "sudden storms." To assert with a straight face that it belonged to Amelia Earhart is stretching possibility to an extraordinary limit.

The claim that the piece of metal found on Nikumaroro is from Amelia Earhart's Lockheed *Electra* is equally ludicrous. Supposedly, it contains "traces" of the manufacturer's labeling.

So far, there are heatedly conflicting analyses of specifications on the metal.

The only possible source in the world for positive identification of parts of Amelia Earhart's aircraft is the manufacturer of that aircraft. No other "expert," individual, organization or institution, either private or governmental, is in possession of the records pertaining specifically to Amelia Earhart's Lockheed *Electra.*

As of this writing, five months after these so-called "discoveries," the manufacturer of Amelia Earhart's aircraft has not even been contacted by TIGHAR, either for information or identification on the piece of metal they found on Nikumaroro Island. *We do not know how any stronger disproof of this hoax can be offered.* Why not go directly to the best source instead of using "secondary experts?"

We believe that the subject piece of metal is only one of thousands of pieces of World War II aircraft to be found on, and in the waters around, most South Pacific islands. This junk, if it would float, has traveled long distances under the force of winds and waves. The type of metal found by TIGHAR was used on thousands of aircraft before World War II and is still being used on aircraft today.

If Amelia and Fred had three days to remove items from the Lockheed *Electra* while it reposed on a reef, they could have removed the entire contents of the airplane. After only a year, the work party put on the island by the British would surely have found a huge array of items and surely reported them to the British, who would have certainly investigated their origin.

We are including the *Electra's* inventory listing shown as "Exhibit M" on the Luke Field, Hawaii military report (**National Archives, Record Group 395**) describing Amelia's groundloop incident. There is no reason to believe that there were any changes in the aircraft's inventory for Amelia's second world flight attempt.

From the inventory, any and all of the following items could have been removed from the plane. Note that many of these items could have been used to help Amelia and Fred obtain food and build a shelter to enable them to survive for more than a few days, surely until the air search reached the island. All this, of course, assumes that Amelia and Fred were uninjured. They could easily have dug-out a huge "SOS" on the sand of the beach, as well as signal passing ships or aircraft.

8. 1 Cloth Sack containing: Chamois Strainer, Cowling Hinges, Grasshopper, Door Handles, 2 Can-o-lites, 12 Dural Plates, Fishing Tackle, Twisted Linen Line, Roll of Tape, Linen, Rubber Hose, Vacuum Line thru Firewall.
10. 2 Two-Cell Ever-ready Flashlights.
15. 1 Bausch & Lomb Field Glasses, 6×30 Serial No. 221939 with carrying case.
22. 1 Nickel plated hand-ax, Marbles No. 2 with Blade Guard.
23. 1 Signal Pistol, No. A-56, Mark III, one inch.
24. 1 Bone Handle, double blade Jack Knife, large Blade No. 22309.
30. 12 Aircraft Water Lights.
33. 14 Signal Pistol Shells.
43. 1 Sun Helmet.
53. 4 Life Preserver Vests, pneumatic.
54. 1 Waterproof zipper bag containing: 4 - 1/2 lb. Nestle chocolate bars, 1 pkg. sipping straws, 6 cans malted milk tablets, 3-1 lb. pkg. raisins, 1 pkg dried apricots, 1 pkg. prunes, 2 cans ripe banana, 3 cans tomato juice, 3 dish towels.
66. 1 Waterproof bag containing: 2 flying suits, 1 raincoat, 1 pr. gloves and 1 pr. shoes. (Authors' note: The shoes may have been either for Amelia or Fred.)
67. 1 Canvas bag containing: 8 ea. No. 2 Unicell Burgess batteries, 1 Waterproof match container with matches, 1 6″ Crescent Adj. wrench, 1 Pr. Glasses type A-1, 1 Tube Cold Cream, 1 spiral notebook, 1 Pr. Thin nose comb pliers, 1 6″ screwdriver, 1 personal letter to R.B. Black, 1 Awl, 1 chamois, 1 bottle Collyrium, 1/4 full, 2 cans 10 Amp. Fuses, 1 Tiger #2 pencil, 1 broken carton absorbent cotton, 1 roll brass wire, 1 roll cord, 1 pkg. containing: 4 - .09 C.P. 11A 122 bulbs and fuses, 2 7/16″ Shackles, 2 spanner wrenches, 2 jack pads.
68. 12 Battery, #935 Ever-ready.
70. 1 First Aid Kit, Bauer & Black No. 42.
71. 2 Thermos Jugs, 1 qt.
75. 1 Tie down rope.

79. 1 Ct. Copperhead diamond matches.
82. 2 Canteens, type 4M.
83. 1 Canteen, type 6M.
87. 2 Pkg. Air Bottles for life jackets.
90. 1 Box Lead Pencils.
100. 3 Scratch Pads.
115. 1 Pencil type flashlight.
125. 2 Parachute flares.

Some of these items are not absolute necessities, but if you have three days to remove them from an aircraft, you may as well take whatever you fancy that might possibly be useful.

SHEET NO. 1
Note: * Items placed in airplane.

No.	Qty.	Unit	Item
1	1	Ea.	Cloth Flying Helmet
2	1	Ea.	One Pound Ball of left twist, type B, 9 cord lock-stitch string
3	1	Ea.	Package containing 23 rolls Pan-chromatic Kodak film, 88 620
4	1	Ea.	Cloth Sack containing: 3 Resistance Bulbs, 3 Cambridge Wools, 1 Pesco Fuel Pump
5	1	Ea.	Cloth Sack containing: 3 Transmitter Tubes, #282 A
6	*1	Ea.	Roll containing: 11 tubes sealed and marked as follows: 3 Bureau of Plant Industry, 8 Office of Cooperative Extension Service, Department of Agriculture, Washington, D.C.
7	1	Ea.	Cloth Sack containing: Soap, Cold Solder, Adhesive Tape
8	1	Ea.	Cloth Sack containing: Chamois Strainer, Cowling Hinges, Grasshopper, Door Handles, 2 Can-o-lites, 12 Dural Plates, Fishing-Tackle, Twisted Linen Line, Roll of Tape Linen, Rubber Hose, Vacuum Line thru Firewall
9	23	Ea.	Unused Lead Seals
10	2	Ea.	Two-Cell Ever-ready Flashlights
11	1	Ea.	Small two-cell Flashlights, made in Japan
12	8	Ea.	Pen size Flashlight Batteries
13	2	Ea.	No. 950 Ever-ready Flashlight Batteries
14	6	Ea.	No. 340 Gem Flashlight Batteries

No.	Qty.	Unit	Item
15	*1	Ea.	Bausch & Lomb Field Glasses, 6x30 Serial No. 221939 with carrying case
16	1	Ea.	Carton, unsealed, marked in pencil "Magneto Parts, Gears and Coils"
17	*1	Ea.	One Quart Fire Extinguisher Pyrene, Serial No. Q-990198, Seal Broken, full of fluid
18	*1	Ea.	Kodak Duo Six-20, lens No. 865715 with carrying case, shutter housing No. 5116031, Film loaded
19	*1	Ea.	Kodak carrying case with Key, Empty (It is believed that Mrs. Putnam has the Kodak in her possession per Lt. Bonner)
20	*3	Ea.	Western Electric Radio Head Phones, type No. 588A (2 equipped with ear cushions)
21	*2	Ea.	Microphones with Cord, Western Electric type No. 631 B
22	1	Ea.	Nickel plated hand-ax, Marbles No. 2 with Blade Guard
23	*1	Ea.	Signal Pistol, No. A-56, Mark III, one inch
24	1	Ea.	Bone Handle, double blade Jack Knife, large Blade No. 22309
25	1	Ea.	Tool Kit containing: —

    1 Ea. PWA-19 Monkey Wrench
    1 Ea. PWA-20 Crescent Wrench
    1 Ea. PWA-21 D.E. Wrench
    1 Ea. PWA-22 D.E. Wrench
    1 Ea. PWA-23 Magneto Wrench
    1 Ea. PWA-24 Socket D.E.
    1 Ea. PWA-28 Rocker Lock
    1 Ea. PWA-29 Screwdriver
    1 Ea. PWA-31 Pliers
    1 Ea. PWA-32 Cold Chisel
    1 Ea. PWA-33 Punch
    1 Ea. PWA-34 Hammer
    1 Ea. PWA-35 Gage
    1 Ea. PWA-36 Kit
    1 Ea. PWA-43 Pliers
    1 Ea. PWA-144 Wrench
    1 Ea. PWA-177 Wrench
    1 Ea. PWA-178 Wrench
    1 Ea. PWA-186 Wrench

No.	Qty.	Unit	Item
			1 Ea. PWA-211 Bag
			1 Ea. PWA-314 Carb. metering jet
			1 Ea. PWA-321 Adjustor
			1 Ea. PWA-439 Wrench
			1 Ea. PWA-455 Depressor
			1 Ea. PWA-459 Depressor
26	*1	Ea.	Tail wheel guide handle
27	1	Ea.	Bundle containing: 1 set refueling pipes, clamps, and hose couplings
28	1	Ea.	Box Kite
29	*1	Pr.	Glasses, type C-2
30	12	Ea.	Aircraft Water Lights
31	*7	Ea.	Aluminum Direction Bombs
32	1	Ea.	5 Watt, 12 Volt Lamp
33	*14	Ea.	Signal Pistol Shells
34	1	Ea.	Detachable door with shade
35	1	Box	Assorted fuses
36	1	Ea.	Cutout Box
37	1	Ea.	Tee Handle Socket Wrench
38	*1	Ea.	Bamboo message passer
39	2	Ea.	Cowl locking pins
40	1	Ea.	Kit containing: 3 Mooring rods, 1 driving rod, and 6 mooring arrows
41	1	Ea.	Grayco lubricating gun, P-600 unit
42	1	Ea.	Canvas, wing catwalk
43	1	Ea.	Sun Helmet
44	1	Ea.	Used Roll friction tape
45	1	Ea.	Tail wheel complete with tire & tube
46	2	Ea.	Floor boards
47	2	Ea.	Flap control covers
48	1	Ea.	Drift meter stand
49	1	Ea.	Anti-glare panel for instrument board
50	1	Ea.	Rubber seat cushion
51	1	Ea.	Carrying case with key containing 14 folders
52	2	Ea.	Red pneumatic cushions
53	4	Ea.	Life Preserver Vests, pneumatic
54	1	Ea.	Waterproof zipper bag containing: 4 - 1/2 lb. nestle chocolate bars, 1 pkg. sipping straws, 6 cans malted milk tablets, 3 - 1 lb. pkg. raisins, 1 pkg. dried apricots, 1 pkg. prunes, 2 cans ripe banana, 3 cans tomato juice, 3 dish towels

No.	Qty.	Unit	Item
55	*1	Ea.	5 lb. can Lubriplate
56	*1	Ea.	10 lb. can Mobilgrease, No. 2
57	*1	Ea.	5 lb. can Mobilgrease, No. 2
58	*1	Ea.	2 Qt. can Lockheed brake fluid
59	1	Ctn.	Spare Propeller bearings
60	*1	Ea.	Base Plate for speed and drift meter
61	1	Pkg.	Rubber vent covers
62	2	Ea.	Cover Plates for wheels
63	1	Ea.	Snap Ring
64	1	Ea.	Control column wheel
65	2	Pcs.	Sheet metal Alcoa
66	1	Ea.	Waterproof bag containing: 2 flying suits, 1 raincoat, 1 pr. gloves and 1 pr. shoes
67	1	Bag	Canvas bag containing: —
			8 Ea. No. 2 Unicell Burgess batteries
			1 Ea. Waterproof match container with matches
			1 Ea. 6" Crescent Adj. wrench
			1 Pr. Glasses type A-1
			1 Tube Cold Cream - 1 spiral notebook
			1 Pr. Thin nose comb. pliers
			1 - 6" screwdriver, 1 personal letter to R.B. Black
			1 Awl, 1 chamois
			1 bottle Collyrium, 1/4 full
			2 cans 10 Amp. Fuses
			1 Tiger #2 pencil
			1 broken carton absorbent cotton
			1 roll brass wire - 1 roll cord
			1 pkg. containing: - 4 ea. .09 C.P. 11A. 122 bulbs and fuses
			2 - 7/16" Shackles, 2 spanner wrenches
			2 jack pads
68	12	Ea.	Battery, #935 Ever-ready
69	100	Ea.	Sipping Straws
70	1	Kit	First Aid, Bauer & Black No. 42
71	2	Ea.	Thermos Jugs, 1 qt.
72	1	Kit	First Aid, "Tabloid," Burroughs Wellcome & Co.
73	*1	Kit	Fire Extinguisher, Pyrene, 1-1/2 qt. Ser. 116610
74	1	Set	Cord, plug and clips, "Cannon A2R"
75	1	Ea.	Tie down rope
76	1	Ea.	Broken container Vortex paper cups

No.	Qty.	Unit	Item
77	1	Ea.	Broken package paper drinking cups
78	1	Ea.	High pressure hand pump, Ser. 799
79	1	Ctn.	Copperhead diamond matches
80	5	Pkg.	Air Travelers chewing gum
81	8	Ea.	1 Qt. Sealright containers
82	2	Ea.	Canteens, type 4 N
83	1	Ea.	Canteens, type 6 N
84	1	Bdl.	Containing: 4 Prop. Blade Covers and 2 engine covers
85	1	Pkg.	Kleenex
86	*1	Ea.	Funnel with chamois strainer
87	1	Pkg.	Air Bottles for life jackets
88	2	Ea.	Fuel tank gauges
89	1	Book	Radio Aids, Navigation
90	1	Box	Lead Pencils
91	1	Book	List of Broadcasting stations
92	2	Book	American Nautical Almanac 1937
93	1	Book	List of Coast Stations & Ship Stations
94	1	Book	List of Aeronautical Stations & Aircraft Stations
95	1	Ea.	List of Stations performing special services
96	2	Ea.	Navigation tables for Mariners and Aviators
97	1	Ea.	Envelope containing miscellaneous navigation papers
98	1	Ea.	Parallel
99	2	Ea.	Dividers
100	3	Ea.	Scratch Pads
101	1	Ea.	Whistle
102	*1	Box	Containing: lights, bulbs, and tubes
103	1	Box	Triangle
104	1	Pkg.	Index Cards
105	1	Ea.	Broken Box Kleenex
106	1	Pkg.	Navigation Charts and airplane log
107	*1	Ea.	Speed & drift indicator, type D-270, with handbook
108	5	Rolls	Miscellaneous maps
109	1	Ea.	Battery container cover
110	2	Ea.	Hose Clamps
111	1	Ea.	Prop. hub nut wrench
112	3	Ea.	Folders with maps
113	*2	Ea.	Lens for cockpit instrument light
114	1	Pc.	Rubber Hose, 1/2″
115	1	Pc.	Pencil type flashlight
116	*1	Ea.	Vibracorder "Ohmer-Kienzle"
117	*4	Ea.	Clocks, Start & Stop "Omega"

No.	Qty.	Unit	Item
118	*1	Ea.	Airspeed Indicator "Pioneer"
119	*1	Ea.	Gage Air Temp. Model 602
120	*1	Ea.	Ammeter, Western 425
121	*1	Ea.	Altimeter, Kohleman, 0 to 20,000
122	*1	Ea.	Pelorus drift sight, MK IIB with extra base
123	*1	Ea.	Straight flight compass
124	1	Ea.	Steamer rug
125	*2	Ea.	Parachute flares

Amelia and Fred could have stretched their food to last a week or so and used their fishing line or picked up shellfish from the lagoon. Water would have been a problem, but do we know that it *didn't* rain during their supposed stay on the island?

One of Gillespie's sources told him he had seen "a water collection device on the island's northern shore in 1944." He would have seen much more than that if Amelia and Fred had been there. Surely there would have been tools and other hard goods from the *Electra's* inventory, unless they were previously removed.

Although Amelia had reportedly removed two parachutes from the aircraft prior to leaving Lae, New Guinea, there is no reason why she would have discarded any of her emergency survival equipment, since she and Fred still faced thousands of miles of open ocean on their way to a remote island.

A few days after Amelia Earhart and Fred Noonan were lost, the U.S. Navy took charge of sea and air search operations. We take exception to Gillespie's assertion that nobody looked in the "most likely place," meaning Nikumaroro. It was, in fact, a most unlikely place, since the likelihood of Amelia flying another 425 miles, low on fuel, was virtually nil.

The battleship *Colorado* was designated to search the water around the Phoenix Atoll group, consisting of nine islands and protruding reefs: Canton, Enderbury, Hull, Birnie, Sydney, Gardner (Nikumaroro), Mkean, Phoenix and Carondelet Reef. Baker Island, located close to Howland in the southeast quadrant, is the only other island in almost 300 miles of open ocean in any direction. Baker Island was searched thoroughly.

Because of the shallow water depths close to the Phoenix Atoll, the battleship *Colorado* cruised offshore in deep water. She launched three scout-observation seaplanes, each with a two-man trained observer crew. Each of these aircraft searched all of the above islands and reefs, overflying them at very low altitude. They reported "no contact" with either Amelia Earhart's downed Lockheed *Electra* or her crew. If one of them reported "signs of recent habitation" (What were these signs, by the way?), they must have been carefully considered and judged to be insignificant.

Having flown air-search missions over open ocean and small islands, we believe that six pair of trained aviation observer eyes were certainly more than adequate to see and observe any signs of life from surviving aviators, not to mention signals from them. No distress signals were ever seen!

Just to be on the safe side, the U.S. Navy minesweeper *Swan*, also in the Phoenix Atoll search area, put ashore a landing party on Canton Island, largest in the Phoenix Group. Again, no trace of the downed fliers or their aircraft was found.

The U.S Navy aircraft carrier *Lexington* launched 58 of her own aircraft in an air search that covered and blocked out 265,000 square miles of sea and islands. Nothing was found.

Aircraft also covered the Gilbert Islands west of Howland, and all the open waters north and east of Howland. It was an extensive combined air and sea search operation, reported to have cost the U.S. government $250,000 per day. Although considered extremely costly at the time, the operation would have cost only slightly more than normal fleet sea and air training exercises conducted periodically, especially during peacetime.

From July 2 through July 18, 1937, the U.S. Coast Guard and the U.S. Navy combed the Pacific for Amelia Earhart without success. Their failure to locate the Lockheed Electra virtually eliminated any further possibility that Amelia and Fred could have reached any safe land.

TIGHAR announced they are planning to return to Nikumaroro Island for another retrieving expedition some day.

We feel this would again prove fruitless. Our analysis of the *Itasca* radio log strongly refutes the possibility that Amelia could have been in any other location except close to Howland Island. This was also the opinion of the *Itasca* Captain.

The China Sighting
Sometime between 1937 and 1945, someone reported seeing Amelia Earhart in China. That story, as others, was of momentary media interest.

Life In New Jersey
As recently as September 1991, newspapers carried articles stating that Amelia Earhart was reported to have been held captive in a prison camp in China until after World War II. She was then returned to the United States under an assumed name given to her by the U.S. Government. The article stated that she died in New Jersey in 1982. No substantiation for this story was provided from any reliable source.

If Amelia were alive in the United States, what would be the purpose in keeping her existence and whereabouts secret for so many years? Amelia loved her well-earned international acclaim, and she would have recaptured it magnificently. She was an accomplished and prolific writer. It would have been extremely difficult for her to live out her days in total anonymity. If Amelia had lived, why didn't she leave behind a chronical of her life after 1937?

The Japanese Intercept
In 1993 a new book appeared titled *Age of Heroes* which was written by Henri Keyser-Andre. Based on his years of Government service in Japan after World War II in the field of commercial aviation, he claims his information concerning the disappearance of Amelia Earhart was obtained from former Japanese military officers and was, in his opinion, 90% factual and 10% logical.

The author concluded that two Japanese military pilots were carefully selected to capture Earhart's plane by using a radio operator who spoke perfect English. By this means, she was to be misdirected in flight, then low on fuel, forced to ditch her Lockheed close to the island of Nonouti located in the Gilbert islands. The Japanese objective was capture of Amelia's aircraft in order to steal its technology by crating and shipping the plane back to the Mitsubishi factory in Japan. Amelia and her navigator Fred Noonan were to be executed and their bodies destroyed so as to leave no trace of their capture.

This so-called "factual" explanation is full of flaws for the following reasons:

1. If Amelia was supposedly maintaining a cruising speed of 125 MPH as suggested by the author, then her aircraft would have passed over the Gilbert islands at approximately 1515 GMT from her takeoff time at Lae, New Guinea at 0000 GMT. That time frame figure translates into 3:15 AM local Gilbert island time after passing two time zones enroute to Howland. Sunrise over the Gilbert's that July 2nd morning was 6:15 AM.

2. The Gilbert chain of islands consists of some sixteen coral islands. Back in 1937 when Amelia Earhart and her navigator Fred Noonan disappeared, the islands were governed by Great Britain as part of the Crown Colony of Gilbert and Ellice islands.

Evaluation Of Facts

We believe that Amelia and her navigator would have had serious second thoughts about changing their flight path in the dark over the Pacific Ocean without absolute verification from the *Itasca*. Since their plan was to reach Howland Island by daylight, a change in flight direction or course, some three hours before sunrise, would have certainly alerted both Amelia and Fred that something was not right. If her navigator had been able to obtain a "star fix," he could have easily determined if they were or were not on course to Howland. The ruse would have been obvious.

Since the Gilbert islands were British territory at the time Amelia Earhart disappeared, it certainly would have been foolish indeed for the Japanese to attempt to occupy and supposedly force her plane down near the offshore waters of Nonouti island. Recovery intact of a downed aircraft, especially the size and weight of a Lockheed *Electra* from offshore waters, would have required many hands along with surface vessels capable of lifting such a heavy load. The time all this would have curtailed along with crating the aircraft parts, could have easily stretched into a week or more. The author of *Age of Heroes* would have you believe that this is exactly what took place, even under the watchful eyes of British Gilbert island citizens who occupied many of the islands at that time.

Co-author Walter Roessler, has personally been involved in a similar aircraft recovery. In 1948, he and two fellow aircraft mechanics were assigned to the task of flying out to a small island some 40 miles West of Puerto Rico in order to disassemble a small single engine aircraft which had crashed while landing on the island. It took three days to remove the wings and prepared the aircraft for loading on a Navy landing craft. It took an additional five Navy personnel to hand drag this aircraft across a coral rock runway and sandy beach in order to reach the landing craft. If it would have been necessary to crate parts of this aircraft, the whole job could have easily stretched into a week of work. This crash, by the way, occurred on a runway and not in offshore waters.

As we pointed out in Chapter 6, the U.S.S. Frigate *Ontario* was on station midway between Lae, New Guinea and Howland Island in order to provide Amelia with both navigation and updated weather data. The *Ontario* was never able to see or hear her aircraft and neither were they able to communicate with Amelia. According to available charts, the *Ontario* was located West of the Gilbert islands. Since Amelia missed making contact with her mid-way check point radio link up, she definitely was nowhere near the Gilbert islands.

The US Coast Guard vessel *Itasca* started a sea search for Amelia's downed aircraft the very same day she failed to arrive at Howland Island. If you examine the search chart of the *Itasca* found in Chapter 6, you will note that the ship searched in and around the Gilbert islands likewise passing close to Nonouti Island, but found no trace of her aircraft or crew. This latest downed aircraft conjecture is not even logical.

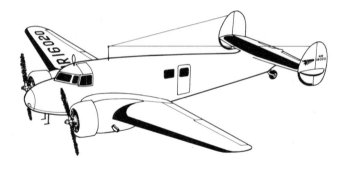

Chapter Nine

AMELIA WAS ONE COURAGEOUS WOMAN
She Did Whatever It Took

What About Amelia's Proficiency?

Looking back over Amelia Earhart's aviation accomplishments, we discovered an unexpected safety record. Initially, it had us questioning her ability to handle airplanes. In her day however, any landing or aborted takeoff attempt was considered successful, as long as you could walk away from it!

The record shows that early in her flying career, Amelia experienced nine incident-mishaps in various types of aircraft; all of which she walked away from! We believe they were caused primarily by a lack of proficiency in the specific type aircraft, and to some degree on weather conditions. Her determination however, enabled her to learn from each situation so she could go forward to her next challenge. She was clearly a lady "on-the-move." She knew what she wanted to do, and she did it.

It's also important to keep in mind that flying back then was not as common or as safe as it is now, and not as much was known about it as is now. Furthermore, many aircraft of the period simply were not as easy to handle as many aircraft are today. Other pilots too, experienced incident-mishaps as they were gaining proficiency. It was just a hazard of the profession. Furthermore, there were no flight simulators back then.

Prior to 1975, aviation authorities were very concerned about severe downdrafts and wind shifts near active airports. It wasn't until June 22, 1975 however, that government regulatory agencies in the United States began to recognize the existence of wind conditions now known as "microbursts and windshears." Pilots had been reporting experiencing severe wind changes and conditions at lower levels during takeoff and landing approach accidents. It was believed that many of those early situations were due to some misunderstood weather phenomena.

On many of Amelia's long distance flights, she encountered challenges in handling her aircraft as well as in navigation, but she never let that stop her from going forward with her plans! She definitely had "a-mind-of-her-own." Nevertheless, she had a habit of operating somewhat with inadequate attention to detail. This eventually forced her to ditch within approximately 50 miles of Howland Island, terminating her life, as well as that of her navigator's.

While further researching Amelia's past flying record we were informed by the NTIS (National Technical Information Service) that there were no individual civilian aircraft accident reports on file earlier than 1965, except those covering commercial air transports. After that date, the NTSB (National Transportation Safety Board) was appointed to investigate and report on all individual, as well as commercial air transport, crashes that fell within their jurisdiction.

That reply to our inquiry certainly indicated Amelia's earlier aircraft crash-incidents or mishaps were apparently never investigated by a recognizable Government Agency. We suspect however that prior to 1965, the Federal Government was involved in air crash investigations of civilian airplanes and maintained records of those investigations.

Some Accident Reports Are "Mysteriously" Missing

In Chapter three we speak of one such case. Two days after Amelia groundlooped her *Electra* on takeoff from Luke Field in Hawaii the morning of March 20, 1937, a Department of Commerce inspector arrived to investigate. Full cooperation on the part of the military was extended to this Federal Inspector and yet, even to this day, his written report of that crash is mysteriously missing from Government files!

We apparently opened a "Pandora's box" when we began researching Amelia's earlier aircraft crash-mishaps. As we reached out for further Government information concerning civilian air crash investigation reports, the Civil Reference Branch of the National Archives in Washington, D.C. advised us that the central files of the Civil Aviation Administration and its predecessor, the Bureau of Air Commerce, are included in record group 273. These are now records of the FAA (Federal Aviation Administration). It was further pointed out that these files are arranged according to a decimal filing scheme in which decimal classification 622.2 covers reports and investigations relating to civilian aircraft accidents.

Unfortunately and somewhat mysteriously, decimal classifications 611 through 671 *are not* in the Government files! We were informed they were removed and apparently destroyed. We have also been advised, that there is nothing in the files that would indicate *why* or *who* removed those records.

It just so happens that files numbered 611 through 671 cover the years 1929 through 1937 which, as far as we have determined, were the years Amelia had most of her crash-mishaps. These were, of course, prior to her fatal crash in the Pacific Ocean on July 2, 1937. File number 622.2 is naturally among the missing records.

We discovered that Amelia has survived some nine (9) aircraft crash-incidents, seven in fixed wing and two in rotary (autogiro) type aircraft from 1921 until 1937. If we count her last crash-mishap into the Pacific Ocean during her 1937 world flight, it would then total ten crashes.

It is not our intent to diminish Amelia Earhart's flying ability or her achievements in the air. It is apparent as pilots though, that if official Government investigations had been conducted into Amelia's previous nine crash-mishaps and possible flight safety standard violations uncovered, she would most likely have been grounded. Also, her planned world flight could either have been canceled or put on hold by the Government regulatory agency then responsible for Air Safety. Since this did not occur, could this then have been a Government cover up? If so, then it had to originate from a very high level of authority. What other reason could there have been to destroy Civil Aviation crash reports covering the years 1929 through 1937 without some official Government explanation.

However you approach this incident, the fact remains that these files are indeed missing and if they had been available in 1937 prior to Amelia's world flight, the proper authorities could have then determined if Amelia's crash-incidents were the result of mechanical or pilot error.

Even after the Federal Government sent their Department of Commerce inspector, Mr. Emil Williams, to investigate Amelia's crash at Luke Field, she was still able to repair her damaged *Electra* and again set out on yet another world flight attempt. The way had been cleared for Amelia to try again, even in the light of her recent crash in Hawaii. Amelia was fortunate to have that type of influence and we suspect that someone was instrumental in removing any official obstacles.

Not only was Amelia cleared to try again to fly around-the-world, but the U.S. Government actually assisted her attempt by providing and preparing a landing strip for her use on tiny Howland Island. In addition, to the U.S.S. frigate *Ontario* stationed midway between Lae, New Guinea and Howland, the Coast Guard ship *Itasca* was on standby at Howland with ground support. This support was undoubtedly furnished because of Amelia's world recognition as a reknown pioneer aviatrix.

Amelia Just Did "Whatever-It-Took!"

Amelia's accidents were either due to her mismanagement of equipment, inadequate proficiency, or very demanding aircraft. Many aircraft of Amelia's time were difficult to handle. They just weren't as refined as the aircraft today.

Another factor was her probable lack of ability to cope with many unusual situations while operating aircraft. Amelia was extremely fortunate to have been able to walk away from all of her crash incidents unscathed, however, the odds against beating a fatal crash were quickly erroding. The number of "close calls" Amelia and her navigator experienced during their world flight are of course not known in their entirety. Furthermore, most pilots, ourselves included, will agree that there had to be more than just a few.

Amelia had her sights fixed on establishing new flying records, especially where no woman had ever flown before. After her marriage to George Putnam, her financial and public relations image were dramatically changed and she was then able to pursue her goals. According to Amelia, the world flight was to be her last record breaking flight; in the end it was and it cost her her life.

Amelia Earhart made at least three ocean crossings in the air. The first was as a passenger in 1928 in the tri-motored float plane which flew from Newfoundland to Ireland. Weather conditions enroute were so bad, that they ended up landing in Burry Port at Southampton in the British Isles.

Determined to go it alone, Amelia flew her Lockheed *Vega* across the Atlantic in 1932. Her destination was to be Paris France, the same as Charles Lindbergh's historic flight in 1927. She was hoping to become the first woman to duplicate that famous flight but due to navigation errors enroute, she became disoriented and was fortunate to be able to land in Londonderry, Ireland.

In 1935 Amelia shipped her Lockheed *Vega* to Hawaii and then flew it back solo to mainland California. This is the only ocean flight she accomplished in which she was able to locate her destination without problems.

These last two ocean crossings by Amelia were accomplished in her single engine *Vega* which she liked to call her "Little Red Bus." This same aircraft is on display at Washington's National Air & Space Museum along with a model of her Lockheed *Electra* NR-16020.

Fig. 9-1. Amelia's "Little Red Bus" now resides in the National Air & Space Museum. A model of her Electra is shown beside it. Roessler photo.

As the ocean crossing flight chart shows, a navigation error on the part of Amelia caused the planned route to Paris, France to throw her off course by several hundred miles. Low on fuel, she sighted and landed her *Vega* in a farmers field in Ireland. This was her first solo Atlantic Ocean flight in 1932.

As previously pointed out and again with this Atlantic Ocean endeavour, navigation was one of the factors that contributed to both Amelia and her navigator's failure to find Howland Island.

During their flight to Dakar, Africa Amelia disagreed with her navigator concerning the course or heading he had instructed her to fly and instead, trusted her own judgment. She ended up some 163 miles off course, landing in St. Louis, Senegal West Africa instead of Dakar.

A navigational error of similar distance while searching for tiny Howland Island after some 20 hours in the air would most likely have resulted in their being lost and disoriented. Noonan's ability to get back on course to Howland likewise failed. It should be noted that a one degree error or variance over 2500 miles of flying (Lae to Howland Island) would result in a 43.6 mile error to the target. A two degree error would compound that to 87.2 miles off course. For the record, a deviation in flight instruments was most likely considered par for the course back in 1937, thus the reason for the deviation card located near the magnetic compass.

Upon examining Amelia's Hawaii-to-California solo flight in 1935, we find that the distance was 2408 miles across the Pacific Ocean. The distance for this flight was some 148 miles less than her planned Lae-to-Howland flight leg.

In her own words she reported somewhere just beyond the halfway position to California, *"Fatigue Increases, I Am Tired."* This clearly indicates she was having difficulty staying awake as well as alert. It can be safely assumed that prior to this flight, Amelia undoubtedly had sufficient rest in Hawaii. Not so on her Lae, New Guinea-to-Howland Island flight two years later. Prior to that leg of her world flight, she and her navigator Fred Noonan had just completed 21,000 miles of flying across twenty-two time zones in 32 days.

Early in Amelia's flying career, she was developing two dangerous habits or signs namely, navigation disorientation and fatigue on long flights. Apparently she herself did not recognize or even consider these conditions as a warning sign. On the long haul of her world flight however, they took their toll. *As we pointed out in previous chapters, there were other contributing factors which played a role in their failed flight but we believe that navigational errors and physical fatigue were the main factors.*

The strongest possible evidence regarding Amelia Earhart's fate appears in the records of the U.S. Coast Guard ship *Itasca* faithfully reproduced earlier in this book. Many people have tried to ignore, change, distort and dismiss the *Itasca's* log. However, it remains a part of military record and history, and it literally speaks for itself!

We not only have the *Itasca* log, but some five years of research and 67 years of aviation experience between us to substantiate our reconstruction of Amelia Earhart's world flight. We believe that no one has previously attempted to solve the mystery of her disappearance from a purely technical viewpoint.

In our summary of the various speculations of Amelia's disappearance, we have not cited many specific details, except in the section covering TIGHAR's recent claims. To do so, would require another book. Our purpose in sharing these stories is to illustrate the public's and media's enduring fascination with the enigma surrounding one of the most famous women in American history.

It would certainly be more satisfying, not to mention sensational, if a more dramatic conclusion of international intrigue could be drawn in ending the Amelia Earhart story. Who knows? With the rapid advance of modern technology, Amelia's *Electra* may one day be recovered from the dispassionate sea.

Rest easy, Amelia Earhart, our "sweetheart-of-the-sky." You did the best you could with the tools you had available. The example of your courage, determination and accomplishments, in the face of incredible odds, lives on as your legacy. You have inspired us to do whatever it takes to pursue our dream; our destiny in life. Keep flying ...

Mike Lowenbein drawing.

COURAGE

Courage is the price that life exacts for granting peace.
The soul that knows it not, knows no release
From little things;

Knows not the livid loneliness of fear
Nor mountain heights, where bitter joy can hear
The sound of wings.

How can life grant us boon of living, compensate
For dull gray ugliness and pregnant hate
Unless we dare

The soul's dominion? Each time we make a choice, we pay
With courage to behold resistless day
And count it fair.
— AMELIA EARHART

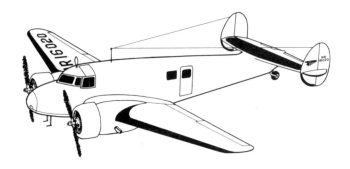

EPILOGUE

In 1949, co-author Walter E. Roessler first met Ms. Clara Livingston, Puerto Rico's most famous woman pilot.

Clara owned a large coconut and grapefruit plantation on the North coast of Puerto Rico called "La Sardinera." Today, this 1600 acres of prime property has been converted to a mostly large tourist area, with two hotels, the Dorado Beach and Cerromar facing the ocean on the North coast of the Island.

At age 25 in 1930, Ms. Livingston became interested in flying and soloed that year. Her aviation and flying career spans some 40 years, including wartime service with the U.S. Army Air Corps. Clara could have become a world famous aviatrix since she had both the flying ability, skill and financial means to accomplish the goal, however she chose a different path. Her military and Civil Air Patrol service were both voluntary and when it came to flying, she was never as far as this co-author knows, "Outside the Envelope."

During his Civil Air Patrol tenure in Puerto Rico from 1949 to 1954, Walter served with Lt. Col. Clara Livingston (she later went on to become the Commanding Officer of the Puerto Rico 52nd Wing). On many occasions, he took off and landed at her Dorado airstrip the many years he lived and served on the island.

Clara, like Amelia, was a dedicated aviatrix. Her friendship with Amelia Earhart spanned many years. While serving with the Civil Air Patrol as a staff officer during the 1953 Ramey

Air Force base encampment, Captain Roessler learned through Col. Livingston, how Amelia had accepted her invitation to stay overnight at her home in Dorado during her world flight stop in Puerto Rico on June 1, 1937.

Clara went on to say that after Amelia had retired for the night, her husband George Putnam called her from the States but Clara told him that Amelia was sleeping; Putnam she recalled, was very displeased. Apparently he had planned for Amelia to stay at the Governor's mansion "La Fortaleza" upon her arrival in Puerto Rico. It would surely have resulted in further publicity for her, but she had other plans.

Amelia had chosen to spend her only evening on the island with a fellow aviatrix as she did with Jackie Cochran prior to the beginning of her world flight. Ms. Livingston expressed many times her pleasure and association with Amelia Earhart, since they had so much in common. That last evening together was spent talking about their flying achievements over the years and of course Amelia's world flight.

Fig. E. Some of the senior members of the Puerto Rico 52nd Wing of the Civil Air Patrol pose for a formal picture during their 1953 Ramey Air Force Base encampment. They are left to right, standing: Capt. Landron, Maj. Denois, Maj. Muniz, Maj. Calvo, *Lt. Col. Clara Livingston*, Maj. Laws, Maj. DeLeon, Maj. Beaudry, Capt. Estava, Lt. Rivera, *Capt. Roessler*. Front row left to right: Lt. Martinez, Lt. Natal, Capt. Martinez, Capt. Audinot, Lt. Rodriquez, Lt. Castrillo and Lt. Sumpter.

The following day Amelia, along with her navigator Fred Noonan, took off for their next stop, *Venezuela*. It was to be the last time Clara Livingston and Amelia Earhart would ever see each other.

Amelia Earhart and Clara Livingston had one thing in common, they both shared the same love of flying, They would have made a terrific team.

Ms. Livingston was the 200th licensed aviatrix in the United States and in addition, the 11th rated woman helicopter pilot. Like Amelia, the sky was her home away from home.

Clara Livingston passed away on January 29, 1992 at Lebanon, New Hampshire. She was 91 years old.

— Walter Roessler

"I know that if I fail or if I am lost you will be blamed for allowing me to leave on this trip; the backers of the flight will be blamed and everyone connected with it. But it's my responsibility and mine alone."

AS AMELIA SAID TO GP THE NIGHT BEFORE (MAY 31, 1937) SHE LEFT MIAMI.

"I have a feeling that there is just about one more good flight left in my system and I hope this trip is it. Anyway when I have finished this job, I mean to give up long-distance 'stunt' flying."

AMELIA SAID THIS TO HERALD TRIBUNE AVIATION CORRESPONDENT CARL ALLEN, WHICH WAS PUBLISHED ON JULY 8, 1937

APPENDIX

About Co-Author Leo F. Gomez

Leo F. Gomez was born in Miami, Florida a mile from the Pan American seaplane base, headquarters for the "Flying Boats" to the Caribbean and South America.

He attended school with children of Pan American pilots. Inside the school lobby were busts of Amelia Earhart and Charles Lindbergh; these famous pioneer aviators reinforced Gomez' love for aviation.

Gomez built model airplanes in his youth, served in the U.S. Navy as an Aviation Machinist Mate, First Class. He is a rated commercial pilot.

He retired after 34 years with Eastern Airlines in the maintenance department, 25 of those as Technical Supervisor. Gomez was an active member of Eastern's new aircraft specification committee for most transport aircraft flying today.

He attended the following technical aviation schools:

1. U.S. Navy Aviation Machinist Mate School, Norfolk, Virginia.
2. Sperry Gyro Auto-Pilot and Instrument School, Brooklyn, NY.
3. Sperry Gyro Auto-Pilot School for current aircraft, Phoenix, AZ.
4. Lockheed PV-1 Ventura and PV-2 Harpoon School, Burbank, CA.
5. Avex Aviation Flying School, Miami, Florida.

While at Eastern Airlines, Gomez was qualified to maintain the following aircraft: DC-3, DC-4, DC-6, DC-7, DC-8, DC-9 Lockheed Constellation, Lockheed Electra II, Lockheed L-1011, Boeing 720, Boeing 727, A-300 Airbus, and the Martin 404.

Leo is now retired and lives with his wife Mary in Sebring, Florida. He is also active in and a past President of the Florida Highlands Chapter 173 of the Air Force Association. Over the years, he has received many awards from the organization including the prestigious Major Thomas B. McGuire Award for his contributions to the AFA and aviation.

About Co-Author Walter E. Roessler

At an early age, Roessler had the privilege to fly with Clarence Chamberlin, the second American aviator to fly across the Atlantic after Lindbergh's historic flight made on May 20-21, 1927. An avid model airplane builder, he attended and graduated from the Manhattan High School of Aviation Trades in New York City. He was also active as a Civil Air Patrol Cadet during the early years of World War II.

After graduation, he enlisted in the Army Air Corps and flew as an air crew member with the 334th Troop Carrier Squadron and 24th Composite Wing of the 6th Air Force. Most if not all of his missions were over the Atlantic and Caribbean Sea. He maintained and crewed in DC-3, B-17, A-20, P-38 and AT-6 type aircraft.

After his military discharge, Roessler attended the Academy of Aeronautics located at LaGuardia Field, Long Island, New York., He is a rated aircraft mechanic and private pilot and has been employed by the Lockheed Aircraft Corporation,

Caribbean Atlantic Airlines and West Indies Airways of Puerto Rico. He continued his Civil Air Patrol service with the 52nd Wing of Puerto Rico from 1949 to 1953 as a rated pilot and Cadet Training Officer.

After retiring to Sebring, Florida in 1980, he was employed as a Fixed Base Operator (FBO) for two Highland County airports. He is also a past President of the Florida Highlands Chapter 173 of the Air Force Association. In 1988, he was awarded the Matty Laird award for his contribution to the enhancement of Aviation in Highlands County.

About Consultant William J. "Bill" Hackett

William J. "Bill" Hackett was born on February 6, 1923 in Orland, Indiana. In 1934, his family moved to Florida, where he heard the call of the skies. He lived only a block from the Pan American seaplane base at Dinner Key in Miami, and near the U.S. Coast Guard Air Station. His ambition to become a naval aviator grew as he watched the "flying boats" arrive daily from South America.

He began his distinguished 30-year military career early in World War II when, in 1942, he joined the U.S. Navy as an aviation cadet. Upon receiving his wings and commission, he was assigned to a dive bomber VB-20 squadron attached to the *U.S.S. Philippine Sea.* In the late 1940's, he piloted naval aircraft in and out of Amelia Earhart Field in Miami. As a navy pilot, he progressed to multi-engine aircraft and performed overwater anti-submarine patrols as pilot-in-command, primarily in the Lockheed P2V Neptune.

Commander Hackett was instrumental in the advancement of aircraft carrier night landings and was the LSO (Landing Signal Officer) on many carriers. As LSO, he received six awards for controlling over 40,000 field carrier landings at Pensacola, Florida Naval Air Station and 2,000 shipboard landings, all without incident. He was named Instructor of the Year in 1956.

During his career, Commander Hackett was qualified to fly 25 different types of aircraft from bi-planes to jets. He was a pilot in four Navy squadrons and was the Aircraft Maintenance Officer aboard the *U.S.S. Wasp.* He also flew as commander of the aircraft permanently assigned to the ship. He instructed students in flying aboard aircraft carriers at the Pensacola Naval Air Station, and he was Officer in Charge of a naval air maintenance school.

Prior to retirement, Commander Hackett flew top echelon naval officers world-wide.

Amelia Earhart Video & Models
Now Available!

Amelia Earhart — The Price of Courage is a biographical sketch of this legendary aviator. It's a fascinating account of her motivations, aspirations, frailties, remarkable courage, and accomplishments. It also covers the amazing publicity machine that kept her in the limelight. It compliments the book very well, and you'll want to view it again-and-again. Contains much rare footage. VHS, Hi-Fi, B/W & Color. Approx. 60 mins. Narrated by actress Kathy Bates.
Order AE Video **$29.95**

Amelia Earhart's Lockheed Electra desktop display model will enhance any office, living room or den. It is made of the finest quality materials available including: select Philippine mahogany, high-tech resins, and precision molded plastic. This is a premium, museum quality, hand-crafted, pre-built model that requires no assembly. Built in 1/48-scale, it has a 12-3/4 inch wingspan, and is 9-5/8 inches long. Comes complete with natural wood display stand. The airplane on the cover of this book is actually the model!
Order Lockheed Electra **$119.95**

Amelia Earhart's Lockheed Vega, her "Little Red Bus," is the one in which she set so many records. The model is **~~SOLD OUT!~~** e of a high quality die-casting in 1/48-scale. It has a wingspan of **~~SOLD OUT~~** nches and is 7-5/8 inches long. The windshield is removable, **SOLD OUT** g a slot in which to insert coins. Comes completely assembled and ready for display. It would enhance any Amelia Earhart fan's home or office.
Order Lockheed Vega **$39.95**

How To Order The Amelia Earhart Video, Models and Additional Books

Telephone Orders: Call (717) 566-0468. Have your VISA or Mastercard ready.

Fax Orders: (717) 566-6423

Postal Orders: AViation Publishers/Markowski International,
One Oakglade Circle, Hummelstown, PA 17036 USA

Please send the following items. I understand I may return any item for a full refund — for any reason, no questions asked.

☐ **Amelia Earhart-Case Closed?** (paperback); $16.95 × qty. = _____

☐ **Amelia Earhart Video-The Price of Courage;** $29.95 × qty. = _____

☐ **Amelia's Lockheed _Electra_ Display Model;** $119.95 × qty. = _____

☐ Please send **FREE catalog** of other aviation items.

Orders for books and videos add postage & handling;   flat rate =   **$4.95**

Orders for either model add postage & handling; $9.95 × qty. = _____

　　　　　　Sub-Total for above items   _____

　　　　　　PA residents add 6% sales tax of above sub-total   _____

　　　　　　TOTAL ENCLOSED FOR ORDER   _____

Name (please print) _____

Address _____

City, State, Zip _____

International Orders: Please double postage and handling figures above, in US funds only drawn against a US bank. Thank you.

Payment:　☐ Check　☐ Money Order　　☐ **Credit Card:**　☐ VISA　☐ MasterCard

Card Number: _____   Exp. Date: _____

Name on Card (please print) _____

SIGNATURE _____

NOTE: Individuals, please check with your local bookstore before ordering any additional books from us. Video & models are not available in bookstores. Quantity discounts available. See below.

QUANTITY SALES: _AMELIA EARHART-CASE CLOSED?_ (paperback or hard-cover), and _AMELIA EARHART-THE PRICE OF COURAGE_ (video) are available at special quantity discounts when purchased in bulk by flying clubs, EAA Chapters, organizations and special interest groups. For details contact:

**AViation Publishers/Markowski International**
One Oakglade Circle
Hummelstown, PA 17036 USA
(717) 566-0468; FAX (717) 566-6423

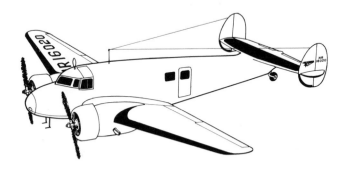